Contents

BRAISED BALSAMIC CHICKEN 6

SALISBURY STEAK 6

SWEET, STICKY AND SPICY CHICKEN 7

ROASTED BRUSSELS SPROUTS 7

BBQ PORK FOR SANDWICHES 8

MARINATED GRILLED SHRIMP 8

SARAH'S APPLESAUCE 9

BAKED HONEY MUSTARD CHICKEN 9

OATMEAL PEANUT BUTTER COOKIES 9

YUMMY HONEY CHICKEN KABOBS 10

ASIAN LETTUCE WRAPS 11

BAKED KALE CHIPS 11

REFRIED BEANS WITHOUT THE REFRY 12

CHICKEN FRIED CHICKEN 12

UNBELIEVABLE CHICKEN 13

MARIE'S EASY SLOW COOKER POT ROAST 13

CHOCOLATE CRINKLES 14

COCKTAIL MEATBALLS 14

PLAYGROUP GRANOLA BARS 15

STUFFED PEPPERS 16

BAKED SLOW COOKER CHICKEN 16

SPANISH RICE 17

CABBAGE ROLL CASSEROLE 17

CHEWY SUGAR COOKIES 18

MMM-MMM BETTER BROWNIES 18

CRANBERRY PISTACHIO BISCOTTI 19

BEST CARROT CAKE EVER 19

OVEN ROASTED POTATOES 20

GRILLED MARINATED SHRIMP 21

MY AMISH FRIEND'S CARAMEL CORN 21

RUTH'S GRANDMA'S PIE CRUST 22

SPICY BEAN SALSA 22

KETTLE CORN 23

EILEEN'S SPICY GINGERBREAD MEN 23

BARBECUED BEEF 24

KUNG PAO CHICKEN 24

SCOTT HIBB'S AMAZING WHISKY GRILLED BABY BACK RIBS 25

FIRECRACKER GRILLED ALASKA SALMON 26

ASIAN BEEF WITH SNOW PEAS 27

HEALTHY BANANA COOKIES 27

BOSTON BAKED BEANS 28

CHARLEY'S SLOW COOKER MEXICAN STYLE MEAT 28

BLACK BEANS AND RICE 29

ROASTED RACK OF LAMB 29

MARINATED PORK TENDERLOIN 30

BLACKENED CHICKEN 31

PEPPERONCINI BEEF 31

CORNISH GAME HENS WITH GARLIC AND ROSEMARY 32

BROOKLYN GIRL'S PENNE ARRABIATA 32

BEST PEANUT BUTTER COOKIES EVER 33

VEGAN BROWNIES 34

MOLASSES SUGAR COOKIES 34

MARINATED TUNA STEAK 35

MOM'S GINGER SNAPS 35

BROCCOLI BEEF 36

BISCOTTI 36

MOLASSES COOKIES 37

PESTO PASTA WITH CHICKEN 37

EASY GUACAMOLE 38

PUMPKIN CAKE 38

CHILI-LIME CHICKEN KABOBS 39

CHEWY PEANUT BUTTER BROWNIES 39

GRILLED BROWN SUGAR PORK CHOPS 40

SALMON WITH BROWN SUGAR GLAZE 40

SNICKERDOODLES 41

CHOCOLATE ZUCCHINI CAKE 41

FRIED CABBAGE 42

VEGAN CHOCOLATE CAKE 42

GRILLED TILAPIA WITH MANGO SALSA 43

SLOW COOKER CHICKEN CACCIATORE 43

FRENCH DIP SANDWICHES 44

BLACK BEAN BROWNIES 44

GRILLED ASPARAGUS 45

PINEAPPLE CHICKEN TENDERS 45

APPLE ENCHILADA DESSERT 46

PAT'S BAKED BEANS 46

GRILLED SHRIMP SCAMPI 47

BLUEBERRY CRUMB BARS 47

SLOW COOKER ADOBO CHICKEN 48

SLOW COOKED CORNED BEEF FOR SANDWICHES 48

SLOW COOKER CRANBERRY PORK 49

KATHY'S DELICIOUS WHOLE SLOW COOKER CHICKEN 49

SESAME NOODLES 49

SLOW COOKER SPICY BLACK-EYED PEAS 50

THE BEST SWEET AND SOUR MEATBALLS 50

EASY MARINATED PORK TENDERLOIN 51

SEARED AHI TUNA STEAKS 51

BREAKFAST SAUSAGE 52

SLOW COOKER BARBEQUE 52

FRESH TOMATO SALSA 53

CINNAMON-ROASTED ALMONDS 53

JAY'S JERK CHICKEN 53

ROASTED LEMON HERB CHICKEN 54

ROAST LEG OF LAMB WITH ROSEMARY 55

BAKED SWEET POTATOES 55

PRIZE WINNING BABY BACK RIBS 56

SLOW COOKER LATIN CHICKEN 56

CHICKPEA CURRY 57

FISH FILLETS ITALIANO 57

SLOW COOKER ROAST BEEF 58

SPICY CHICKEN BREASTS 58

GINGER VEGGIE STIR-FRY 59

BAKED BEANS 59

BEST GUACAMOLE 60

PEPPERMINT MERINGUES 60

SESAME GREEN BEANS 60

EASY HERB ROASTED TURKEY 61

ROAST PORK WITH MAPLE AND MUSTARD GLAZE 61

BEST BEEF DIP EVER 62

VICKI'S HUSH PUPPIES 62

HOUSE FRIED RICE 62

BUFFALO CHICKEN FINGERS 63

MARRAKESH VEGETABLE CURRY 64

PECAN PIE BARS 64

GNOCCHI 65

CHICKEN IN A POT 65

WHOLE WHEAT AND HONEY PIZZA DOUGH 66

DIVINE HARD-BOILED EGGS 66

SIMPLE COUNTRY RIBS 67

PEANUT NOODLES 67

GRILLED ASIAN CHICKEN 68

BARBEQUED MARINATED FLANK STEAK 68

SNICKERDOODLES 69

YAKISOBA CHICKEN 69

FAVORITE PEANUT BUTTER COOKIES 70

LONDON BROIL 70

ASIAN BEEF SKEWERS 71

FRIED RICE 71

PICO DE GALLO 72

PORCUPINES 72

EASIEST POT ROAST EVER 73

MUSHROOM SLOW COOKER ROAST BEEF 73

ANGEL FOOD CAKE 74

BARBEQUED RIBS 74

QUICK GNOCCHI 75

MEDITERRANEAN LEMON CHICKEN 75

PERFECT SUSHI RICE 76

ROSEMARY BRAISED LAMB SHANKS 76

ONION RICE 77

APRICOT CHICKEN 77

GRILLED ROCK LOBSTER TAILS 78

GRILLED PORTOBELLO MUSHROOMS 78

ORANGE CHICKEN STIR FRY 78

EASY GRILLED CHICKEN TERIYAKI 79

MICROWAVE CARAMEL POPCORN 79

VEGGIE POT PIE 80

THREE BERRY PIE 81

GRECIAN PORK TENDERLOIN 81

GRANDMA'S GINGERSNAPS 82

SLOW COOKER HONEY GARLIC CHICKEN 82

CHICKEN LO MEIN 83

QUICK AND EASY PANCIT 84

BARBEQUE PORK TWO WAYS 84

LENTILS AND SPINACH 85

EGG IN A HOLE 85

ESPINACAS CON GARBANZOS (SPINACH WITH GARBANZO BEANS) 86

RONALDO'S BEEF CARNITAS 86

VEGAN BEAN TACO FILLING 87

SUKHOTHAI PAD THAI 87

SWEET AND SOUR MEATBALLS 88

PUTTANESCA 88

CHINESE CHICKEN FRIED RICE 89

GINGERBREAD BISCOTTI 89

CANDIED ALMONDS 90

ZESTY PORCUPINE MEATBALLS 90

ISLAND KIELBASA IN A SLOW COOKER 91

SPICED SLOW COOKER APPLESAUCE 91

BRAZILIAN WHITE RICE 92

TOFU AND VEGGIES IN PEANUT SAUCE 92

APPLE BUNDT CAKE 92

SLOW COOKER GREEN BEANS, HAM AND POTATOES 93

GRILLED SALMON 94

BOW TIE PASTA WITH SAUSAGE AND SWEET PEPPERS 94

AMERICAN CHOP SUEY 95

FRIED OKRA 95

RAMJAM CHICKEN 96

BRAISED BALSAMIC CHICKEN

Servings: 6 | Prep: 10m | Cooks: 25m | Total: 35m

NUTRITION FACTS

Calories: 196 | Carbohydrates: 7.6g | Fat: 7g | Protein: 23.8g | Cholesterol: 61mg

INGREDIENTS

- 6 skinless, boneless chicken breast halves
- 1/2 cup balsamic vinegar
- 1 teaspoon garlic salt
- 1 teaspoon dried basil
- ground black pepper to taste
- 1 teaspoon dried oregano
- 2 tablespoons olive oil
- 1 teaspoon dried rosemary
- 1 onion, thinly sliced
- 1/2 teaspoon dried thyme
- 1 (14.5 ounce) can diced tomatoes

DIRECTIONS

1. Season both sides of chicken breasts with garlic salt and pepper.

2. Heat olive oil in a skillet over medium heat; cook seasoned chicken breasts until chicken is browned, 3 to 4 minutes per side. Add onion; cook and stir until onion is browned, 3 to 4 minutes.

3. Pour diced tomatoes and balsamic vinegar over chicken; season with basil, oregano, rosemary and thyme. Simmer until chicken is no longer pink and the juices run clear, about 15 minutes. An instant-read thermometer inserted into the center should read at least 165 degrees F (74 degrees C).

SALISBURY STEAK

Servings: 6 | Prep: 20m | Cooks: 20m | Total: 40m

NUTRITION FACTS

Calories: 440 | Carbohydrates: 14.1g | Fat: 32.3g | Protein: 23g | Cholesterol: 127mg

INGREDIENTS

- 1 (10.5 ounce) can condensed French onion soup
- 1 tablespoon all-purpose flour
- 1 1/2 pounds ground beef
- 1/4 cup ketchup
- 1/2 cup dry bread crumbs
- 1/4 cup water
- 1 egg
- 1 tablespoon Worcestershire sauce
- 1/4 teaspoon salt
- 1/2 teaspoon mustard powder
- 1/8 teaspoon ground black pepper

DIRECTIONS

1. In a large bowl, mix together 1/3 cup condensed French onion soup with ground beef, bread crumbs, egg, salt and black pepper. Shape into 6 oval patties.
2. In a large skillet over medium-high heat, brown both sides of patties. Pour off excess fat.
3. In a small bowl, blend flour and remaining soup until smooth. Mix in ketchup, water, Worcestershire sauce and mustard powder. Pour over meat in skillet. Cover, and cook for 20 minutes, stirring occasionally.

SWEET, STICKY AND SPICY CHICKEN
Servings: 4 | Prep: 10m | Cooks: 12m | Total: 22m

NUTRITION FACTS
Calories: 232 | Carbohydrates: 13.9g | Fat: 9.3g | Protein: 22.8g | Cholesterol: 59mg

INGREDIENTS
- 1 tablespoon brown sugar
- 2 tablespoons hot sauce
- 2 tablespoons honey
- salt and pepper to taste
- 1/4 cup soy sauce
- 4 skinless, boneless chicken breast halves - cut into 1/2 inch strips
- 2 teaspoons chopped fresh ginger root
- 1 tablespoon vegetable oil
- 2 teaspoons chopped garlic

DIRECTIONS

1. Mix together brown sugar, honey, soy sauce, ginger, garlic and hot sauce in a small bowl.
2. Lightly salt and pepper the chicken strips.
3. Heat oil in a large skillet over medium heat. Add chicken strips and brown on both sides, about 1 minute per side. Pour the sauce over the chicken. Simmer uncovered until the sauce thickens, 8 to 10 minutes.

ROASTED BRUSSELS SPROUTS
Servings: 6 | Prep: 15m | Cooks: 45m | Total: 1h

NUTRITION FACTS
Calories: 104 | Carbohydrates: 10g | Fat: 7.3g | Protein: 2.9g | Cholesterol: 0mg

INGREDIENTS
- 1 1/2 pounds Brussels sprouts, ends trimmed and yellow leaves removed
- 1 teaspoon kosher salt
- 3 tablespoons olive oil
- 1/2 teaspoon freshly ground black pepper

DIRECTIONS
1. Preheat oven to 400 degrees F (205 degrees C).
2. Place trimmed Brussels sprouts, olive oil, kosher salt, and pepper in a large resealable plastic bag. Seal tightly, and shake to coat. Pour onto a baking sheet, and place on center oven rack.

3. Roast in the preheated oven for 30 to 45 minutes, shaking pan every 5 to 7 minutes for even browning. Reduce heat when necessary to prevent burning. Brussels sprouts should be darkest brown, almost black, when done. Adjust seasoning with kosher salt, if necessary. Serve immediately.

BBQ PORK FOR SANDWICHES
Servings: 12 | Prep: 15m | Cooks: 4h30m | Total: 4h45m

NUTRITION FACTS

Calories: 355 | Carbohydrates: 15.2g | Fat: 18.1g | Protein: 30.2g | Cholesterol: 83mg

INGREDIENTS

- 1 (14 ounce) can beef broth
- 1 (18 ounce) bottle barbeque sauce
- 3 pounds boneless pork ribs

DIRECTIONS

1. Pour can of beef broth into slow cooker, and add boneless pork ribs. Cook on High heat for 4 hours, or until meat shreds easily. Remove meat, and shred with two forks. It will seem that it's not working right away, but it will.
2. Preheat oven to 350 degrees F (175 degrees C). Transfer the shredded pork to a Dutch oven or iron skillet, and stir in barbeque sauce.
3. Bake in the preheated oven for 30 minutes, or until heated through.

MARINATED GRILLED SHRIMP
Servings: 6 | Prep: 15m | Cooks: 6m | Total: 55m

NUTRITION FACTS

Calories: 273 | Carbohydrates: 2.8g | Fat: 14.7g | Protein: 31g | Cholesterol: 230mg

INGREDIENTS

- 3 cloves garlic, minced
- 1/2 teaspoon salt
- 1/3 cup olive oil
- 1/4 teaspoon cayenne pepper
- 1/4 cup tomato sauce
- 2 pounds fresh shrimp, peeled and deveined
- 2 tablespoons red wine vinegar
- skewers
- 2 tablespoons chopped fresh basil

DIRECTIONS

1. In a large bowl, stir together the garlic, olive oil, tomato sauce, and red wine vinegar. Season with basil, salt, and cayenne pepper. Add shrimp to the bowl, and stir until evenly coated. Cover, and refrigerate for 30 minutes to 1 hour, stirring once or twice.
2. Preheat grill for medium heat. Thread shrimp onto skewers, piercing once near the tail and once near the head. Discard marinade.

3. Lightly oil grill grate. Cook shrimp on preheated grill for 2 to 3 minutes per side, or until opaque.

SARAH'S APPLESAUCE
Servings: 4 | Prep: 10m | Cooks: 20m | Total: 30m

NUTRITION FACTS
Calories: 121 | Carbohydrates: 31.8g | Fat: 0.2g | Protein: 0.4g | Cholesterol: 0mg

INGREDIENTS
- 4 apples - peeled, cored and chopped
- 1/4 cup white sugar
- 3/4 cup water
- 1/2 teaspoon ground cinnamon

DIRECTIONS

1. In a saucepan, combine apples, water, sugar, and cinnamon. Cover, and cook over medium heat for 15 to 20 minutes, or until apples are soft. Allow to cool, then mash with a fork or potato masher.

BAKED HONEY MUSTARD CHICKEN
Servings: 6 | Prep: 15m | Cooks: 45m | Total: 1h

NUTRITION FACTS
Calories: 232 | Carbohydrates: 24.8g | Fat: 3.7g | Protein: 25.6g | Cholesterol: 67mg

INGREDIENTS
- 6 skinless, boneless chicken breast halves
- 1 teaspoon dried basil
- salt and pepper to taste
- 1 teaspoon paprika
- 1/2 cup honey
- 1/2 teaspoon dried parsley
- 1/2 cup prepared mustard

DIRECTIONS

1. Preheat oven to 350 degrees F (175 degrees C).
2. Sprinkle chicken breasts with salt and pepper to taste, and place in a lightly greased 9x13 inch baking dish. In a small bowl, combine the honey, mustard, basil, paprika, and parsley. Mix well. Pour 1/2 of this mixture over the chicken, and brush to cover.
3. Bake in the preheated oven for 30 minutes. Turn chicken pieces over and brush with the remaining 1/2 of the honey mustard mixture. Bake for an additional 10 to 15 minutes, or until chicken is no longer pink and juices run clear. Let cool 10 minutes before serving.

OATMEAL PEANUT BUTTER COOKIES
Servings: 48 | Prep: 15m | Cooks: 15m | Total: 1h | Additional: 30m

NUTRITION FACTS

Calories: 120 | Carbohydrates: 12.8g | Fat: 7.1g | Protein: 2.3g | Cholesterol: 8mg

INGREDIENTS

- 1/2 cup shortening
- 2 eggs
- 1/2 cup margarine, softened
- 1 1/2 cups all-purpose flour
- 1 cup packed brown sugar
- 2 teaspoons baking soda
- 3/4 cup white sugar
- 1 teaspoon salt
- 1 cup peanut butter
- 1 cup quick-cooking oats

DIRECTIONS

1. Preheat oven to 350 degrees F (175 degrees C).

2. In a large bowl, cream together shortening, margarine, brown sugar, white sugar, and peanut butter until smooth. Beat in the eggs one at a time until well blended. Combine the flour, baking soda, and salt; stir into the creamed mixture. Mix in the oats until just combined. Drop by teaspoonfuls onto ungreased cookie sheets.

3. Bake for 10 to 15 minutes in the preheated oven, or until just light brown. Don't over-bake. Cool and store in an airtight container.

YUMMY HONEY CHICKEN KABOBS

Servings: 12 | Prep: 15m | Cooks: 15m | Total: 2h30m | Additional: 2h

NUTRITION FACTS

Calories: 178 | Carbohydrates: 12.4g | Fat: 6.6g | Protein: 17.4g | Cholesterol: 45mg

INGREDIENTS

- 1/4 cup vegetable oil
- 2 cloves garlic
- 1/3 cup honey
- 5 small onions, cut into 2 inch pieces
- 1/cup soy sauce
- 2 red bell peppers, cut into 2 inch pieces
- 1/4 teaspoon ground black pepper
- skewers
- 8 skinless, boneless chicken breast halves - cut into 1 inch cubes

DIRECTIONS

1. In a large bowl, whisk together oil, honey, soy sauce, and pepper. Before adding chicken, reserve a small amount of marinade to brush onto kabobs while cooking. Place the chicken, garlic, onions and peppers in the bowl, and marinate in the refrigerator at least 2 hours (the longer the better).

2. Preheat the grill for high heat.

3. Drain marinade from the chicken and vegetables, and discard marinade. Thread chicken and vegetables alternately onto the skewers.

4. Lightly oil the grill grate. Place the skewers on the grill. Cook for 12 to 15 minutes, until chicken juices run clear. Turn and brush with reserved marinade frequently.

ASIAN LETTUCE WRAPS

Servings: 4 | Prep: 20m | Cooks: 15m | Total: 35m

NUTRITION FACTS

Calories: 388 | Carbohydrates: 24.3g | Fat: 22.3g | Protein: 23.4g | Cholesterol: 69mg

INGREDIENTS

- 16 Boston Bibb or butter lettuce leaves
- 1 tablespoon rice wine vinegar
- 1 pound lean ground beef
- 2 teaspoons minced pickled ginger
- 1 tablespoon cooking oil
- 1 dash Asian chile pepper sauce, or to taste (optional)
- 1 large onion, chopped
- 1 (8 ounce) can water chestnuts, drained and finely chopped
- 1/4 cup hoisin sauce
- 1 bunch green onions, chopped
- 2 cloves fresh garlic, minced
- 2 teaspoons Asian (dark) sesame oil
- 1 tablespoon soy sauce

DIRECTIONS

1. Rinse whole lettuce leaves and pat dry, being careful not tear them. Set aside.
2. Heat a large skillet over medium-high heat. Cook and stir beef and cooking oil in the hot skillet until browned and crumbly, 5 to 7 minutes. Drain and discard grease; transfer beef to a bowl. Cook and stir onion in the same skillet used for beef until slightly tender, 5 to 10 minutes. Stir hoisin sauce, garlic, soy sauce, vinegar, ginger, and chile pepper sauce into onions. Add water chestnuts, green onions, sesame oil, and cooked beef; cook and stir until the onions just begin to wilt, about 2 minutes.
3. Arrange lettuce leaves around the outer edge of a large serving platter and pile meat mixture in the center.

BAKED KALE CHIPS

Servings: 6 | Prep: 10m | Cooks: 10m | Total: 20m

NUTRITION FACTS

Calories: 58 | Carbohydrates: 7.6g | Fat: 2.8g | Protein: 2.5g | Cholesterol: 0mg

INGREDIENTS

- 1 bunch kale
- 1 teaspoon seasoned salt

- 1 tablespoon olive oil

DIRECTIONS

1. Preheat an oven to 350 degrees F (175 degrees C). Line a non insulated cookie sheet with parchment paper.
2. With a knife or kitchen shears carefully remove the leaves from the thick stems and tear into bite size pieces. Wash and thoroughly dry kale with a salad spinner. Drizzle kale with olive oil and sprinkle with seasoning salt.
3. Bake until the edges brown but are not burnt, 10 to 15 minutes.

REFRIED BEANS WITHOUT THE REFRY
Servings: 15 | Prep: 15m | Cooks: 8h | Total: 8h15m

NUTRITION FACTS

Calories: 139 | Carbohydrates: 25.4g | Fat: 0.5g | Protein: 8.5g | Cholesterol: 0mg

INGREDIENTS

- 1 onion, peeled and halved
- 5 teaspoons salt
- 3 cups dry pinto beans, rinsed
- 1 3/4 teaspoons fresh ground black pepper
- 1/2 fresh jalapeno pepper, seeded and chopped
- 1/8 teaspoon ground cumin, optional
- 2 tablespoons minced garlic
- 9 cups water

DIRECTIONS

1. Place the onion, rinsed beans, jalapeno, garlic, salt, pepper, and cumin into a slow cooker. Pour in the water and stir to combine. Cook on High for 8 hours, adding more water as needed. Note: if more than 1 cup of water has evaporated during cooking, then the temperature is too high.
2. Once the beans have cooked, strain them, and reserve the liquid. Mash the beans with a potato masher, adding the reserved water as needed to attain desired consistency.

CHICKEN FRIED CHICKEN
Servings: 6 | Prep: 25m | Cooks: 20m | Total: 45m

NUTRITION FACTS

Calories: 887 | Carbohydrates: 14.2g | Fat: 79.6g | Protein: 29.2g | Cholesterol: 103mg

INGREDIENTS

- 30 saltine crackers
- 1/2 teaspoon ground black pepper
- 2 tablespoons all-purpose flour
- 1 egg
- 2 tablespoons dry potato flakes
- 6 skinless, boneless chicken breast halves
- 1 teaspoon seasoned salt
- 2 cups vegetable oil for frying

DIRECTIONS

1. Place crackers in a large resealable plastic bag; seal bag and crush crackers with a rolling pin until they are coarse crumbs. Add the flour, potato flakes, seasoned salt, and pepper and mix well.
2. Beat egg in a shallow dish or bowl. One by one, dredge chicken pieces in egg, then place in bag with crumb mixture. Seal bag and shake to coat.
3. Heat oil in a deep-fryer or large saucepan to 350 degrees F (175 degrees C).
4. Fry chicken, turning frequently, until golden brown and juices run clear, 15 to 20 minutes.

UNBELIEVABLE CHICKEN

Servings: 6 | Prep: 15m | Cooks: 20m | Total: 9h | Additional: 8h25m

NUTRITION FACTS

Calories: 337 | Carbohydrates: 22.4 | Fat: 16.4g | Protein: 24.8g | Cholesterol: 67mg

INGREDIENTS

- 1/4 cup cider vinegar
- 1/2 cup brown sugar
- 3 tablespoons prepared coarse-ground mustard
- 1 1/2 teaspoons salt
- 3 cloves garlic, peeled and minced
- ground black pepper to taste
- 1 lime, juiced
- 6 tablespoons olive oil
- 1/2 lemon, juiced
- 6 skinless, boneless chicken breast halves

DIRECTIONS

1. In a large glass bowl, mix the cider vinegar, mustard, garlic, lime juice, lemon juice, brown sugar, salt, and pepper. Whisk in the olive oil. Place chicken in the mixture. Cover, and marinate 8 hours, or overnight.
2. Preheat an outdoor grill for high heat.
3. Lightly oil the grill grate. Place chicken on the prepared grill, and cook 6 to 8 minutes per side, until juices run clear. Discard marinade.

MARIE'S EASY SLOW COOKER POT ROAST

Servings: 8 | Prep: 40m | Cooks: 9h | Total: 9h40m

NUTRITION FACTS

Calories: 540 | Carbohydrates: 18.2g | Fat: 30.6g | Protein: 45.7g | Cholesterol: 147mg

INGREDIENTS

- 4 pounds chuck roast
- 3 carrots, chopped
- salt and pepper to taste

- 1 onion, chopped
- 1 packet dry onion soup mix
- 3 potatoes, peeled and cubed
- 1 cup water
- 1 stalk celery, chopped

DIRECTIONS

1. Season the roast with salt and pepper to taste. Brown on all sides in a large skillet over high heat, about 4 minutes per side.

2. Place the roast in the slow cooker and add the soup mix, water, carrots, onion, potatoes, and celery.

3. Cover and cook on Low setting for 8 to 10 hours.

CHOCOLATE CRINKLES

Servings: 72 | Prep: 20m | Cooks: 12m | Total: 5h | Additional: 4h28m

NUTRITION FACTS

Calories: 58 | Carbohydrates: 9.8g | Fat: 2g | Protein: 0.9g | Cholesterol: 10mg

INGREDIENTS

- 1 cup unsweetened cocoa powder
- 2 cups all-purpose flour
- 2 cups white sugar
- 2 teaspoons baking powder
- 1/2 cup vegetable oil
- 1/2 teaspoon salt
- 4 eggs
- 1/2 cup confectioners' sugar
- 2 teaspoons vanilla extract

DIRECTIONS

1. In a medium bowl, mix together cocoa, white sugar, and vegetable oil. Beat in eggs one at a time, then stir in the vanilla. Combine the flour, baking powder, and salt; stir into the cocoa mixture. Cover dough, and chill for at least 4 hours.

2. Preheat oven to 350 degrees F (175 degrees C). Line cookie sheets with parchment paper. Roll dough into one inch balls. I like to use a number 50 size scoop. Coat each ball in confectioners' sugar before placing onto prepared cookie sheets.

3. Bake in preheated oven for 10 to 12 minutes. Let stand on the cookie sheet for a minute before transferring to wire racks to cool.

COCKTAIL MEATBALLS

Servings: 10 | Prep: 20m | Cooks: 1h25m | Total: 1h45m

NUTRITION FACTS

Calories: 193 | Carbohydrates: 15.2g | Fat: 10.2g | Protein: 9.8g | Cholesterol: 53mg

INGREDIENTS

- 1 pound lean ground beef

- 1 (8 ounce) can jellied cranberry sauce
- 1 egg
- 3/4 cup chili sauce
- 2 tablespoons water
- 1 tablespoon brown sugar
- 1/2 cup bread crumbs
- 1 1/2 teaspoons lemon juice
- 3 tablespoons minced onion

DIRECTIONS

1. Preheat oven to 350 degrees F (175 degrees C).
2. In a large bowl, mix together the ground beef, egg, water, bread crumbs, and minced onion. Roll into small meatballs.
3. Bake in preheated oven for 20 to 25 minutes, turning once.
4. In a slow cooker or large saucepan over low heat, blend the cranberry sauce, chili sauce, brown sugar, and lemon juice. Add meatballs, and simmer for 1 hour before serving.

PLAYGROUP GRANOLA BARS

Servings: 24 | Prep: 15m | Cooks: 35m | Total: 50m

NUTRITION FACTS

Calories: 161 | Carbohydrates: 26.6g | Fat: 5.5g | Protein: 2.4g | Cholesterol: 8mg

INGREDIENTS

- 2 cups rolled oats
- 3/4 teaspoon salt
- 3/4 cup packed brown sugar
- 1/2 cup honey
- 1/2 cup wheat germ
- 1 egg, beaten
- 3/4 teaspoon ground cinnamon
- 1/2 cup vegetable oil
- 1 cup all-purpose flour
- 2 teaspoons vanilla extract
- 3/4 cup raisins (optional)

DIRECTIONS

1. Preheat the oven to 350 degrees F (175 degrees C). Generously grease a 9x13 inch baking pan.
2. In a large bowl, mix together the oats, brown sugar, wheat germ, cinnamon, flour, raisins and salt. Make a well in the center, and pour in the honey, egg, oil and vanilla. Mix well using your hands. Pat the mixture evenly into the prepared pan.
3. Bake for 30 to 35 minutes in the preheated oven, until the bars begin to turn golden at the edges. Cool for 5 minutes, then cut into bars while still warm. Do not allow the bars to cool completely before cutting, or they will be too hard to cut.

STUFFED PEPPERS

Servings: 6 | Prep: 20m | Cooks: 1h | Total: 1h20m

NUTRITION FACTS

Calories: 248 | Carbohydrates: 25.6g | Fat: 9.4g | Protein: 16g | Cholesterol: 46mg

INGREDIENTS

- 1 pound ground beef
- 1 tablespoon Worcestershire sauce
- 1/2 cup uncooked long grain white rice
- 1/4 teaspoon garlic powder
- 1 cup water
- 1/4 teaspoon onion powder
- 6 green bell peppers
- salt and pepper to taste
- 2 (8 ounce) cans tomato sauce
- 1 teaspoon Italian seasoning

DIRECTIONS

1. Preheat oven to 350 degrees F (175 degrees C).
2. Place the rice and water in a saucepan, and bring to a boil. Reduce heat, cover, and cook 20 minutes. In a skillet over medium heat, cook the beef until evenly browned.
3. Remove and discard the tops, seeds, and membranes of the bell peppers. Arrange peppers in a baking dish with the hollowed sides facing upward. (Slice the bottoms of the peppers if necessary so that they will stand upright.)
4. In a bowl, mix the browned beef, cooked rice, 1 can tomato sauce, Worcestershire sauce, garlic powder, onion powder, salt, and pepper. Spoon an equal amount of the mixture into each hollowed pepper. Mix the remaining tomato sauce and Italian seasoning in a bowl, and pour over the stuffed peppers.
5. Bake 1 hour in the preheated oven, basting with sauce every 15 minutes, until the peppers are tender.

BAKED SLOW COOKER CHICKEN

Servings: 6 | Prep: 20m | Cooks: 10h | Total: 10h20m

NUTRITION FACTS

Calories: 408 | Carbohydrates: 0.2g | Fat: 28.5g | Protein: 35.2g | Cholesterol: 142mg

INGREDIENTS

- 1 (2 to 3 pound) whole chicken
- 1 teaspoon paprika
- salt and pepper to taste

DIRECTIONS

1. Wad three pieces of aluminum foil into 3 to 4 inch balls, and place them in the bottom of the slow cooker.
2. Rinse the chicken, inside and out, under cold running water. Pat dry with paper towels. Season the chicken with the salt, pepper and paprika, and place in the slow cooker on top of the crumpled aluminum foil.

3. Set the slow cooker to High for 1 hour, then turn down to Low for about 8 to 10 hours, or until the chicken is no longer pink and the juices run clear.

SPANISH RICE
Servings: 4 | Prep: 10m | Cooks: 30m | Total: 40m

NUTRITION FACTS

Calories: 270 | Carbohydrates: 45.7g | Fat: 7.6g | Protein: 4.8g | Cholesterol: 0mg

INGREDIENTS

- 2 tablespoons vegetable oil
- 2 cups water
- 1 cup uncooked white rice
- 1 (10 ounce) can diced tomatoes and green chiles
- 1 onion, chopped
- 2 teaspoons chili powder, or to taste
- 1/2 green bell pepper, chopped
- 1 teaspoon salt

DIRECTIONS

1. Heat oil in a deep skillet over medium heat. Saute rice, onion, and bell pepper until rice is browned and onions are tender.

2. Stir in water and tomatoes. Season with chili powder and salt. Cover, and simmer for 30 minutes, or until rice is cooked and liquid is absorbed.

CABBAGE ROLL CASSEROLE
Servings: 12 | Prep: 10m | Cooks: 1h30m | Total: 1h40m

NUTRITION FACTS

Calories: 352 | Carbohydrates: 25.5g | Fat: 20.6g | Protein: 17.1g | Cholesterol: 64mg

INGREDIENTS

- 2 pounds ground beef
- 1 cup uncooked white rice
- 1 cup chopped onion
- 1 teaspoon salt
- 1 (29 ounce) can tomato sauce
- 2 (14 ounce) cans beef broth
- 3 1/2 pounds chopped cabbage

DIRECTIONS

1. Preheat oven to 350 degrees F (175 degrees C).
2. In a large skillet, brown beef in oil over medium high heat until redness is gone. Drain off fat.
3. In a large mixing bowl combine the onion, tomato sauce, cabbage, rice and salt. Add meat and mix all together. Pour mixture into a 9x13 inch baking dish. Pour broth over meat mixture and bake in the preheated oven, covered, for 1 hour. Stir, replace cover and bake for another 30 minutes.

CHEWY SUGAR COOKIES

Servings: 30 | Prep: 10m | Cooks: 10m | Total: 1h25m | Additional: 1h5m

NUTRITION FACTS

Calories: 172 | Carbohydrates: 23.9g | Fat: 7.9g | Protein: 1.7g | Cholesterol: 12mg

INGREDIENTS

- 2 3/4 cups all-purpose flour
- 2 cups white sugar
- 1 teaspoon baking soda
- 2 eggs
- 1/2 teaspoon salt
- 2 teaspoons vanilla extract
- 1 1/4 cups margarine
- 1/4 cup white sugar for decoration

DIRECTIONS

1. Preheat the oven to 350 degrees F (175 degrees C). In a medium bowl, stir together the flour, baking soda, and salt; set aside.
2. In a large bowl, cream together the margarine and 2 cups sugar until light and fluffy. Beat in the eggs one at a time, then the vanilla. Gradually stir in the dry ingredients until just blended.
3. Wrap dough with plastic wrap and chill for 30 minutes to 1 hour.
4. Roll the dough into walnut-sized balls and roll the balls in remaining 1/4 cup of sugar. Place cookies 2 inches apart onto ungreased cookie sheets and flatten slightly.
5. Bake for 8 to 10 minutes in the preheated oven, until lightly browned at the edges. Allow cookies to cool on baking sheet for 5 minutes before removing to a wire rack to cool completely.

MMM-MMM BETTER BROWNIES

Servings: 16 | Prep: 15m | Cooks: 25m | Total: 40m

NUTRITION FACTS

Calories: 161 | Carbohydrates: 17.1g | Fat: 10.2g | Protein: 2.1g | Cholesterol: 23mg

INGREDIENTS

- 1/2 cup vegetable oil
- 1/3 cup unsweetened cocoa powder
- 1 cup white sugar
- 1/4 teaspoon baking powder
- 1 teaspoon vanilla extract
- 1/4 teaspoon salt
- 2 eggs
- 1/2 cup chopped walnuts (optional)
- 1/2 cup all-purpose flour

DIRECTIONS

1. Preheat oven to 350 degrees F (175 degrees C). Grease a 9x9 inch baking pan.

2. In a medium bowl, mix together the oil, sugar, and vanilla. Beat in eggs. Combine flour, cocoa, baking powder, and salt; gradually stir into the egg mixture until well blended. Stir in walnuts, if desired. Spread the batter evenly into the prepared pan.

3. Bake for 20 to 25 minutes, or until the brownie begins to pull away from edges of pan. Let cool on a wire rack before cutting into squares.

CRANBERRY PISTACHIO BISCOTTI

Servings: 36 | Prep: 25m | Cooks: 45m | Total: 1h20m | Additional: 10m

NUTRITION FACTS

Calories: 92 | Carbohydrates: 11.7g | Fat: 4.3g | Protein: 2.1g | Cholesterol: 10mg

INGREDIENTS

- 1/4 cup light olive oil
- 13/4 cups all-purpose flour
- 3/4 cup white sugar
- 1/4 teaspoon salt
- 2 teaspoons vanilla extract
- 1 teaspoon baking powder
- 1/2 teaspoon almond extract
- 1/2 cup dried cranberries
- 2 eggs
- 1 1/2 cups pistachio nuts

DIRECTIONS

1. Preheat the oven to 300 degrees F (150 degrees C).

2. In a large bowl, mix together oil and sugar until well blended. Mix in the vanilla and almond extracts, then beat in the eggs. Combine flour, salt, and baking powder; gradually stir into egg mixture. Mix in cranberries and nuts by hand.

3. Divide dough in half. Form two logs (12x2 inches) on a cookie sheet that has been lined with parchment paper. Dough may be sticky; wet hands with cool water to handle dough more easily.

4. Bake for 35 minutes in the preheated oven, or until logs are light brown. Remove from oven, and set aside to cool for 10 minutes. Reduce oven heat to 275 degrees F (135 degrees C).

5. Cut logs on diagonal into 3/4 inch thick slices. Lay on sides on parchment covered cookie sheet. Bake approximately 8 to 10 minutes, or until dry; cool.

BEST CARROT CAKE EVER

Servings: 16 | Prep: 1h30m | Cooks: 1h | Total: 2h30m

NUTRITION FACTS

Calories: 457 | Carbohydrates: 66.3g | Fat: 20.2g | Protein: 5.9g | Cholesterol: 47mg

INGREDIENTS

- 6 cups grated carrots

- 1 cup crushed pineapple, drained
- 1 cup brown sugar
- 3 cups all-purpose flour
- 1 cup raisins
- 1 ½ teaspoons baking soda
- 4 eggs
- 1 teaspoon salt
- 1 1/2 cups white sugar
- 4 teaspoons ground cinnamon
- 1 cup vegetable oil
- 1 cup chopped walnuts
- 2 teaspoons vanilla extract

DIRECTIONS

1. In a medium bowl, combine grated carrots and brown sugar. Set aside for 60 minutes, then stir in raisins.
2. Preheat oven to 350 degrees F (175 degrees C). Grease and flour two 10 inch cake pans.
3. In a large bowl, beat eggs until light. Gradually beat in the white sugar, oil and vanilla. Stir in the pineapple. Combine the flour, baking soda, salt and cinnamon, stir into the wet mixture until absorbed. Finally stir in the carrot mixture and the walnuts. Pour evenly into the prepared pans.
4. Bake for 45 to 50 minutes in the preheated oven, until cake tests done with a toothpick. Cool for 10 minutes before removing from pan. When completely cooled, frost with cream cheese frosting.

OVEN ROASTED POTATOES

Servings: 4 | Prep: 15m | Cooks: 30m | Total: 45m

NUTRITION FACTS

Calories: 289 | Carbohydrates: 53.1g | Fat: 7.1g | Protein: 5 g | Cholesterol: 0mg

INGREDIENTS

- 1/8 cup olive oil
- 1/2 teaspoon dried oregano
- 1 tablespoon minced garlic
- 1/2 teaspoon dried parsley
- 1/2 teaspoon dried basil
- 1/2 teaspoon crushed red pepper flakes
- 1/2 teaspoon dried marjoram
- 1/2 teaspoon salt
- 1/2 teaspoon dried dill weed
- 4 large potatoes, peeled and cubed
- 1/2 teaspoon dried thyme

DIRECTIONS

1. Preheat oven to 475 degrees F (245 degrees C).

2. In a large bowl, combine oil, garlic, basil, marjoram, dill weed, thyme, oregano, parsley, red pepper flakes, and salt. Stir in potatoes until evenly coated. Place potatoes in a single layer on a roasting pan or baking sheet.

3. Roast for 20 to 30 minutes in the preheated oven, turning occasionally to brown on all sides.

GRILLED MARINATED SHRIMP
Servings: 6 | Prep: 30m | Cooks: 10m | Total: 2h40m

NUTRITION FACTS
Calories: 447 | Carbohydrates: 3.7g | Fat: 37.5g | Protein: 25.3g | Cholesterol: 230mg

INGREDIENTS
- 1 cup olive oil
- 2 teaspoons dried oregano
- 1/4 cup chopped fresh parsley
- 1 teaspoon salt
- 1 lemon, juiced
- 1 teaspoon ground black pepper
- 2 tablespoons hot pepper sauce
- 2 pounds large shrimp, peeled and deveined with tails attached
- 3 cloves garlic, minced
- skewers
- 1 tablespoon tomato paste

DIRECTIONS

1. In a mixing bowl, mix together olive oil, parsley, lemon juice, hot sauce, garlic, tomato paste, oregano, salt, and black pepper. Reserve a small amount for basting later. Pour remaining marinade into a large resealable plastic bag with shrimp. Seal, and marinate in the refrigerator for 2 hours.
2. Preheat grill for medium-low heat. Thread shrimp onto skewers, piercing once near the tail and once near the head. Discard marinade.
3. Lightly oil grill grate. Cook shrimp for 5 minutes per side, or until opaque, basting frequently with reserved marinade.

MY AMISH FRIEND'S CARAMEL CORN
Servings: 28 | Prep: 15m | Cooks: 1h | Total: 1h15m

NUTRITION FACTS
Calories: 238 | Carbohydrates: 21.9g | Fat: 16.3g | Protein: 3.4g | Cholesterol: 0mg

INGREDIENTS
- 7 quarts plain popped popcorn
- 1 teaspoon salt
- 2 cups dry roasted peanuts (optional)
- 1 cup margarine
- 2 cups brown sugar
- 1/2 teaspoon baking soda
- 1/2 cup light corn syrup
- 1 teaspoon vanilla extract

DIRECTIONS

1. Place the popped popcorn into two shallow greased baking pans. You may use roasting pans, jelly roll pans, or disposable roasting pans. Add the peanuts to the popped corn if using. Set aside.
2. Preheat the oven to 250 degrees F (120 degrees C). Combine the brown sugar, corn syrup, margarine and salt in a saucepan. Bring to a boil over medium heat, stirring enough to blend. Once the mixture begins to boil, boil for 5 minutes while stirring constantly.
3. Remove from the heat, and stir in the baking soda and vanilla. The mixture will be light and foamy. Immediately pour over the popcorn in the pans, and stir to coat. Don't worry too much at this point about getting all of the corn coated.
4. Bake for 1 hour, removing the pans, and giving them each a good stir every 15 minutes. Line the counter top with waxed paper. Dump the corn out onto the waxed paper and separate the pieces. Allow to cool completely, then store in airtight containers or resealable bags.

RUTH'S GRANDMA'S PIE CRUST
Servings: 32 | Prep: 10m | Cooks: 10m | Total: 32m

NUTRITION FACTS
Calories: 163 | Carbohydrates: 13.1g | Fat: 11.5g | Protein: 1.8g | Cholesterol: 6mg

INGREDIENTS
- 4 cups all-purpose flour
- 2 teaspoons salt
- 1 3/4 cups shortening
- 1 egg
- 3 tablespoons white sugar
- 1/2 cup water

DIRECTIONS

1. In a large mixing bowl, combine all-purpose flour, shortening, sugar, and salt. Blend together with a pastry cutter until crumbly.
2. In a small bowl, mix egg with water. Blend into flour mixture. Chill in refrigerator until ready to use.

SPICY BEAN SALSA
Servings: 12 | Prep: 10m | Cooks: 8h | Total: 8h10m

NUTRITION FACTS
Calories: 155 | Carbohydrates: 20.4g | Fat: 6.4g | Protein: 5g | Cholesterol: 0mg

INGREDIENTS
- 1 (15 ounce) can black-eyed peas
- 1 (4 ounce) can diced jalapeno peppers
- 1 (15 ounce) can black beans, rinsed and drained
- 1 (14.5 ounce) can diced tomatoes, drained
- 1 (15 ounce) can whole kernel corn, drained
- 1 cup Italian-style salad dressing
- 1/2 cup chopped onion

- 1/2 teaspoon garlic salt
- 1/2 cup chopped green bell pepper

DIRECTIONS

1. In a medium bowl, combine black-eyed peas, black beans, corn, onion, green bell pepper, jalapeno peppers and tomatoes. Season with Italian-style salad dressing and garlic salt; mix well. Cover, and refrigerate overnight to blend flavors.

KETTLE CORN

Servings: 5 | Prep: 15m | Cooks: 15m | Total: 20m

NUTRITION FACTS

Calories: 209 | Carbohydrates: 24.8g | Fat: 11.9g | Protein: 2.4g | Cholesterol: 0mg

INGREDIENTS

- 1/4 cup vegetable oil
- 1/2 cup unpopped popcorn kernels
- 1/4 cup white sugar

DIRECTIONS

1. Heat the vegetable oil in a large pot over medium heat. Once hot, stir in the sugar and popcorn. Cover, and shake the pot constantly to keep the sugar from burning. Once the popping has slowed to once every 2 to 3 seconds, remove the pot from the heat and continue to shake for a few minutes until the popping has stopped. Pour into a large bowl, and allow to cool, stirring occasionally to break up large clumps.

EILEEN'S SPICY GINGERBREAD MEN

Servings: 30 | Prep: 20m | Cooks: 10m | Total: 30m

NUTRITION FACTS

Calories: 88 | Carbohydrates: 14g | Fat: 3.3g | Protein: 1g | Cholesterol: 7mg

INGREDIENTS

- 1/2 cup margarine
- 1/2 teaspoon baking powder
- 1/2 cup sugar
- 1/2 teaspoon baking soda
- 1/2 cup molasses
- 1/2 teaspoon ground cinnamon
- 1 egg yolk
- 1 teaspoon ground cloves
- 2 cups sifted all-purpose flour
- 1 teaspoon ginger
- 1/2 teaspoon salt
- 1/2 teaspoon ground nutmeg

DIRECTIONS

1. In a large bowl, cream together the margarine and sugar until smooth. Stir in molasses and egg yolk. Combine the flour, salt, baking powder, baking soda, cinnamon, cloves, ginger, and nutmeg; blend into the molasses mixture until smooth. Cover, and chill for at least one hour.
2. Preheat the oven to 350 degrees F (175 degrees C). On a lightly floured surface, roll the dough out to 1/4 inch thickness. Cut into desired shapes with cookie cutters. Place cookies 2 inches apart on ungreased cookie sheets.
3. Bake for 8 to 10 minutes in the preheated oven, until firm. Remove from cookie sheets to cool on wire racks. Frost or decorate when cool.

BARBECUED BEEF
Servings: 12 | Prep: 20m | Cooks: 10h | Total: 10h20m
NUTRITION FACTS
Calories: 276 | Carbohydrates: 13.5g | Fat: 16.2g | Protein: 18.7g | Cholesterol: 65mg
INGREDIENTS
- 1 1/2 cups ketchup
- 1 teaspoon liquid smoke flavoring
- 1/4 cup packed brown sugar
- 1/2 teaspoon salt
- 1/4 cup red wine vinegar
- 1/4 teaspoon ground black pepper
- 2 tablespoons prepared Dijon-style mustard
- 1/4 teaspoon garlic powder
- 2 tablespoons Worcestershire sauce
- 1 (4 pound) boneless chuck roast

DIRECTIONS

1. In a large bowl, combine ketchup, brown sugar, red wine vinegar, Dijon-style mustard, Worcestershire sauce, and liquid smoke. Stir in salt, pepper, and garlic powder.
2. Place chuck roast in a slow cooker. Pour ketchup mixture over chuck roast. Cover, and cook on Low for 8 to 10 hours.
3. Remove chuck roast from slow cooker, shred with a fork, and return to the slow cooker. Stir meat to evenly coat with sauce. Continue cooking approximately 1 hour.

KUNG PAO CHICKEN
Servings: 4 | Prep: 30m | Cooks: 30m | Total: 1h30m | Additional: 30m
NUTRITION FACTS
Calories: 437 | Carbohydrates: 25.3g | Fat: 23.3g | Protein: 34.4g | Cholesterol: 66mg
INGREDIENTS
- 1 pound skinless, boneless chicken breast halves - cut into chunks
- 1 teaspoon distilled white vinegar
- 2 tablespoons white wine
- 2 teaspoons brown sugar

- 2 tablespoons soy sauce
- 4 green onions, chopped
- 2 tablespoons sesame oil, divided
- 1 tablespoon chopped garlic
- 2 tablespoons cornstarch, dissolved in 2 tablespoons water
- 1 (8 ounce) can water chestnuts
- 1 ounce hot chile paste
- 4 ounces chopped peanuts

DIRECTIONS

1. To Make Marinade: Combine 1 tablespoon wine, 1 tablespoon soy sauce, 1 tablespoon oil and 1 tablespoon cornstarch/water mixture and mix together. Place chicken pieces in a glass dish or bowl and add marinade. Toss to coat. Cover dish and place in refrigerator for about 30 minutes.

2. To Make Sauce: In a small bowl combine 1 tablespoon wine, 1 tablespoon soy sauce, 1 tablespoon oil, 1 tablespoon cornstarch/water mixture, chili paste, vinegar and sugar. Mix together and add green onion, garlic, water chestnuts and peanuts. In a medium skillet, heat sauce slowly until aromatic.

3. Meanwhile, remove chicken from marinade and saute in a large skillet until meat is white and juices run clear. When sauce is aromatic, add sauteed chicken to it and let simmer together until sauce thickens.

SCOTT HIBB'S AMAZING WHISKY GRILLED BABY BACK RIBS

Servings: 4 | Prep: 20m | Cooks: 2h40m | Total: 3h

NUTRITION FACTS

Calories: 1029 | Carbohydrates: 52.8g | Fat: 68g | Protein: 50.2g | Cholesterol: 234mg

INGREDIENTS

- 2 (2 pound) slabs baby back pork ribs
- 2 tablespoons Worcestershire sauce
- coarsely ground black pepper
- 2 teaspoons salt
- 1 tablespoon ground red chile pepper
- 1/4 teaspoon coarsely ground black pepper
- 2 1/4 tablespoons vegetable oil
- 1 1/4 teaspoons liquid smoke flavoring
- 1/2 cup minced onion
- 2 teaspoons whiskey
- 1 1/2 cups water
- 2 teaspoons garlic powder
- 1/2 cup tomato paste
- 1/4 teaspoon paprika
- 1/2 cup white vinegar

- 1/2 teaspoon onion powder
- 1/2 cup brown sugar
- 1 tablespoon dark molasses
- 2 1/2 tablespoons honey
- 1/2 tablespoon ground red chile pepper

DIRECTIONS

1. Preheat oven to 300 degree F (150 degrees C).
2. Cut each full rack of ribs in half, so that you have 4 half racks. Sprinkle salt and pepper (more pepper than salt), and 1 tablespoon chile pepper over meat. Wrap each half rack in aluminum foil. Bake for 2 1/2 hours.
3. Meanwhile, heat oil in a medium saucepan over medium heat. Cook and stir the onions in oil for 5 minutes. Stir in water, tomato paste, vinegar, brown sugar, honey, and Worcestershire sauce. Season with 2 teaspoons salt, 1/4 teaspoon black pepper, liquid smoke, whiskey, garlic powder, paprika, onion powder, dark molasses, and 1/2 tablespoon ground chile pepper. Bring mixture to a boil, then reduce heat. Simmer for 1 1/4 hours, uncovered, or until sauce thickens. Remove from heat, and set sauce aside.
4. Preheat an outdoor grill for high heat.
5. Remove the ribs from the oven, and let stand 10 minutes. Remove the racks from the foil, and place on the grill. Grill the ribs for 3 to 4 minutes on each side. Brush sauce on the ribs while they're grilling, just before you serve them (adding it too early will burn it).

FIRECRACKER GRILLED ALASKA SALMON

Servings: 8 | Prep: 20m | Cooks: 20m | Total: 6h40m

NUTRITION FACTS

Calories: 307 | Carbohydrates: 4.6g | Fat: 21.5g | Protein: 23.3g | Cholesterol: 63mg

INGREDIENTS

- 8 (4 ounce) fillets salmon
- 2 cloves garlic, minced
- 1/2 cup peanut oil
- 1 1/2 teaspoons ground ginger
- 4 tablespoons soy sauce
- 2 teaspoons crushed red pepper flakes
- 4 tablespoons balsamic vinegar
- 1 teaspoon sesame oil
- 4 tablespoons green onions, chopped
- 1/2 teaspoon salt
- 3 teaspoons brown sugar

DIRECTIONS

1. Place salmon filets in a medium, nonporous glass dish. In a separate medium bowl, combine the peanut oil, soy sauce, vinegar, green onions, brown sugar, garlic, ginger, red pepper flakes, sesame oil and salt. Whisk together well, and pour over the fish. Cover and marinate the fish in the refrigerator for 4 to 6 hours.
2. Prepare an outdoor grill with coals about 5 inches from the grate, and lightly oil the grate.
3. Grill the fillets 5 inches from coals for 10 minutes per inch of thickness, measured at the thickest part, or until fish just flakes with a fork. Turn over halfway through cooking.

ASIAN BEEF WITH SNOW PEAS
Servings: 4 | Prep: 5m | Cooks: 10m | Total: 15m

NUTRITION FACTS
Calories: 203 | Carbohydrates: 9.7g | Fat: 10g | Protein: 16g | Cholesterol: 39mg

INGREDIENTS
- 3 tablespoons soy sauce
- 1 tablespoon minced fresh ginger root
- 2 tablespoons rice wine
- 1 tablespoon minced garlic
- 1 tablespoon brown sugar
- 1 pound beef round steak, cut into thin strips
- 1/2 teaspoon cornstarch
- 8 ounces snow peas
- 1 tablespoon vegetable oil

DIRECTIONS
1. In a small bowl, combine the soy sauce, rice wine, brown sugar and cornstarch. Set aside.
2. Heat oil in a wok or skillet over medium high heat. Stir-fry ginger and garlic for 30 seconds. Add the steak and stir-fry for 2 minutes or until evenly browned. Add the snow peas and stir-fry for an additional 3 minutes. Add the soy sauce mixture, bring to a boil, stirring constantly. Lower heat and simmer until the sauce is thick and smooth. Serve immediately.

HEALTHY BANANA COOKIES
Servings: 36 | Prep: 15m | Cooks: 20m | Total: 50m | Additional: 15m

NUTRITION FACTS
Calories: 56 | Carbohydrates: 8.4g | Fat: 2.4g | Protein: 0.8g | Cholesterol: 0mg

INGREDIENTS
- 3 ripe bananas
- 1/3 cup vegetable oil
- 2 cups rolled oats
- 1 teaspoon vanilla extract
- 1 cup dates, pitted and chopped

DIRECTIONS

1. Preheat oven to 350 degrees F (175 degrees C).

2. In a large bowl, mash the bananas. Stir in oats, dates, oil, and vanilla. Mix well, and allow to sit for 15 minutes. Drop by teaspoonfuls onto an ungreased cookie sheet.

3. Bake for 20 minutes in the preheated oven, or until lightly brown.

BOSTON BAKED BEANS

Servings: 6 | Prep: 30m | Cooks: 4h | Total: 5h | Additional: 30m

NUTRITION FACTS

Calories: 382 | Carbohydrates: 63.1g | Fat: 6.3g | Protein: 20.7g | Cholesterol: 14mg

INGREDIENTS

- 2 cups navy beans
- 1/4 teaspoon ground black pepper
- 1/2 pound bacon
- 1/4 teaspoon dry mustard
- 1 onion, finely diced
- 1/2 cup ketchup
- 3 tablespoons molasses
- 1 tablespoon Worcestershire sauce
- 2 teaspoons salt
- 1/4 cup brown sugar

DIRECTIONS

1. Soak beans overnight in cold water. Simmer the beans in the same water until tender, approximately 1 to 2 hours. Drain and reserve the liquid.

2. Preheat oven to 325 degrees F (165 degrees C).

3. Arrange the beans in a 2 quart bean pot or casserole dish by placing a portion of the beans in the bottom of dish, and layering them with bacon and onion.

4. In a saucepan, combine molasses, salt, pepper, dry mustard, ketchup, Worcestershire sauce and brown sugar. Bring the mixture to a boil and pour over beans. Pour in just enough of the reserved bean water to cover the beans. Cover the dish with a lid or aluminum foil.

5. Bake for 3 to 4 hours in the preheated oven, until beans are tender. Remove the lid about halfway through cooking, and add more liquid if necessary to prevent the beans from getting too dry.

CHARLEY'S SLOW COOKER MEXICAN STYLE MEAT

Servings: 12 | Prep: 30m | Cooks: 8h | Total: 8h50m

NUTRITION FACTS

Calories: 260 | Carbohydrates: 3.3g | Fat: 19.1g | Protein: 18.4g | Cholesterol: 69mg

INGREDIENTS

- 1 (4 pound) chuck roast
- 1 1/4 cups diced green chile pepper
- 1 teaspoon salt
- 1 teaspoon chili powder

- 1 teaspoon ground black pepper
- 1 teaspoon ground cayenne pepper
- 2 tablespoons olive oil
- 1 (5 ounce) bottle hot pepper sauce
- 1 large onion, chopped
- 1 teaspoon garlic powder

DIRECTIONS

1. Trim the roast of any excess fat, and season with salt and pepper. Heat olive oil in a large skillet over medium-high heat. Place the beef in the hot skillet, and brown it quickly on all sides.
2. Transfer the roast to a slow cooker and top it with the chopped onion. Season with chile peppers, chili powder, cayenne pepper, hot pepper sauce, and garlic powder. Add enough water to cover 1/3 of the roast.
3. Cover, and cook on High for 6 hours, checking to make sure there is always at least a small amount of liquid in the bottom of the cooker. Reduce heat to Low, and continue cooking for 2 to 4 hours, or until meat is totally tender and falls apart.
4. Transfer the roast to a bowl and shred it using two forks (reserve 2 cups of cooking liquid, if desired). Serve in tacos or burritos (see Cook's Note).

BLACK BEANS AND RICE

Servings: 10 | Prep: 5m | Cooks: 25m | Total: 30m

NUTRITION FACTS

Calories: 140 | Carbohydrates: 27.1g | Fat: 0.9g | Protein: 6.3g | Cholesterol: 0mg

INGREDIENTS

- 1 teaspoon olive oil
- 1 1/2 cups low sodium, low fat vegetable broth
- 1 onion, chopped
- 1 teaspoon ground cumin
- 2 cloves garlic, minced
- 1/4 teaspoon cayenne pepper
- 3/4 cup uncooked white rice
- 3 1/2 cups canned black beans, drained

DIRECTIONS

1. In a stockpot over medium-high heat, heat the oil. Add the onion and garlic and saute for 4 minutes. Add the rice and saute for 2 minutes.
2. Add the vegetable broth, bring to a boil, cover and lower the heat and cook for 20 minutes. Add the spices and black beans.

ROASTED RACK OF LAMB

Servings: 4 | Prep: 20m | Cooks: 20m | Total: 40m

NUTRITION FACTS

Calories: 481 | Carbohydrates: 5.6g | Fat: 40.8g | Protein: 22.2g | Cholesterol: 94mg

INGREDIENTS

- 1/2 cup fresh bread crumbs
- 1 (7 bone) rack of lamb, trimmed and frenched

- 2 tablespoons minced garlic
- 1 teaspoon salt
- 2 tablespoons chopped fresh rosemary
- 1 teaspoon black pepper
- 1 teaspoon salt
- 2 tablespoons olive oil
- 1/4 teaspoon black pepper
- 1 tablespoon Dijon mustard
- 2 tablespoons olive oil

DIRECTIONS

1. Preheat oven to 450 degrees F (230 degrees C). Move oven rack to the center position.
2. In a large bowl, combine bread crumbs, garlic, rosemary, 1 teaspoon salt and 1/4 teaspoon pepper. Toss in 2 tablespoons olive oil to moisten mixture. Set aside.
3. Season the rack all over with salt and pepper. Heat 2 tablespoons olive oil in a large heavy oven proof skillet over high heat. Sear rack of lamb for 1 to 2 minutes on all sides. Set aside for a few minutes. Brush rack of lamb with the mustard. Roll in the bread crumb mixture until evenly coated. Cover the ends of the bones with foil to prevent charring.
4. Arrange the rack bone side down in the skillet. Roast the lamb in preheated oven for 12 to 18 minutes, depending on the degree of doneness you want. With a meat thermometer, take a reading in the center of the meat after 10 to 12 minutes and remove the meat, or let it cook longer, to your taste. Let it rest for 5 to 7 minutes, loosely covered, before carving between the ribs.

MARINATED PORK TENDERLOIN

Servings: 4 | Prep: 10m | Cooks: 20m | Total: 6h30m | Additional: 6h

NUTRITION FACTS

Calories: 278 | Carbohydrates: 16.9g | Fat: 10.7g | Protein: 27g | Cholesterol: 73mg

INGREDIENTS

- 1/4 cup soy sauce
- 1 teaspoon ground cinnamon
- 1/4 cup packed brown sugar
- 2 tablespoons olive oil
- 2 tablespoons sherry
- 1 pinch garlic powder
- 1 1/2 teaspoons dried minced onion
- 2 (3/4 pound) pork tenderloins

DIRECTIONS

1. Place soy sauce, brown sugar, sherry, dried onion, cinnamon, olive oil, and a touch of garlic powder in a large resealable plastic bag. Seal, and shake to mix. Place pork in bag with marinade, seal, and refrigerate for 6 to 12 hours.
2. Preheat grill for high heat.
3. Lightly oil grate. Place tenderloins on grill, and discard marinade. Cook 20 minutes, or to desired doneness. Slice into medallions, and serve.

BLACKENED CHICKEN

Servings: 2 | Prep: 10m | Cooks: 10m | Total: 20m

NUTRITION FACTS

Calories: 135 | Carbohydrates: 0.9g | Fat: 3g | Protein: 24.7g | Cholesterol: 67mg

INGREDIENTS

- 1/2 teaspoon paprika
- 1/4 teaspoon dried thyme
- 1/8 teaspoon salt
- 1/8 teaspoon ground white pepper
- 1/4 teaspoon cayenne pepper
- 1/8 teaspoon onion powder
- 1/4 teaspoon ground cumin
- 2 skinless, boneless chicken breast halves

DIRECTIONS

1. Preheat oven to 350 degrees F (175 degrees C). Lightly grease a baking sheet. Heat a cast iron skillet over high heat for 5 minutes until it is smoking hot.
2. Mix together the paprika, salt, cayenne, cumin, thyme, white pepper, and onion powder. Oil the chicken breasts with cooking spray on both sides, then coat the chicken breasts evenly with the spice mixture.
3. Place the chicken in the hot pan, and cook for 1 minute. Turn, and cook 1 minute on other side. Place the breasts on the prepared baking sheet.
4. Bake in the preheated oven until no longer pink in the center and the juices run clear, about 5 minutes.

PEPPERONCINI BEEF

Servings: 8 | Prep: 10m | Cooks: 8h | Total: 8h20m

NUTRITION FACTS

Calories: 998 | Carbohydrates: 71.5g | Fat: 52.7g | Protein: 55.9g | Cholesterol: 160mg

INGREDIENTS

- 1 (3 pound) beef chuck roast
- 8 hoagie rolls, split lengthwise
- 4 cloves garlic, sliced
- 16 slices provolone cheese
- 1 (16 ounce) jar pepperoncini

DIRECTIONS

1. Make small cuts in roast, and insert garlic slices in cuts. Place roast in the slow cooker, and pour the entire contents of the jar of pepperoncini, including liquid, over meat.
2. Cover, and cook on Low for 6 to 8 hours.
3. When making the sandwiches, place meat in rolls, top with cheese, and zap in a microwave for a few seconds. Don't forget to use the pepperoncini in the sandwiches!

CORNISH GAME HENS WITH GARLIC AND ROSEMARY
Servings: 4 | Prep: 20m | Cooks: 1h | Total: 1h20m

NUTRITION FACTS

Calories: 814 | Carbohydrates: 9.7g | Fat: 57.5g | Protein: 59.4g | Cholesterol: 340mg

INGREDIENTS

- 4 Cornish game hens
- 24 cloves garlic
- salt and pepper to taste
- 1/3 cup white wine
- 1 lemon, quartered
- 1/3 cup low-sodium chicken broth
- 4 sprigs fresh rosemary
- 4 sprigs fresh rosemary, for garnish
- 3 tablespoons olive oil

DIRECTIONS

1. Preheat oven to 450 degrees F (230 degrees C).
2. Rub hens with 1 tablespoon of the olive oil. Lightly season hens with salt and pepper. Place 1 lemon wedge and 1 sprig rosemary in cavity of each hen. Arrange in a large, heavy roasting pan, and arrange garlic cloves around hens. Roast in preheated oven for 25 minutes.
3. Reduce oven temperature to 350 degrees F (175 degrees C). In a mixing bowl, whisk together wine, chicken broth, and remaining 2 tablespoons of oil; pour over hens. Continue roasting about 25 minutes longer, or until hens are golden brown and juices run clear. Baste with pan juices every 10 minutes.
4. Transfer hens to a platter, pouring any cavity juices into the roasting pan. Tent hens with aluminum foil to keep warm. Transfer pan juices and garlic cloves to a medium saucepan and boil until liquids reduce to a sauce consistency, about 6 minutes. Cut hens in half lengthwise and arrange on plates. Spoon sauce and garlic around hens. Garnish with rosemary sprigs, and serve.

BROOKLYN GIRL'S PENNE ARRABIATA
Servings: 6 | Prep: 20m | Cooks: 25m | Total: 45m

NUTRITION FACTS

Calories: 588 | Carbohydrates: 75.3g | Fat: 16.5g | Protein: 33.6g | Cholesterol: 108mg

INGREDIENTS

- 1/2 cup olive oil, divided
- 2 eggs
- 6 cloves garlic, sliced
- 2 cups bread crumbs
- 1 teaspoon red pepper flakes
- 1 teaspoon garlic powder
- 1 (28 ounce) can diced tomatoes with garlic and olive oil

- 1 teaspoon salt
- 1/2 cup tomato sauce
- 1 teaspoon pepper
- 1 bunch fresh basil, chopped
- 1 pound thin chicken breast cutlets
- 1 (12 ounce) package dried penne pasta

DIRECTIONS

1. Heat 1/4 cup of olive oil in a large skillet over medium heat. Add the garlic, and saute for a few minutes. Sprinkle in the red pepper flakes, and saute for another minute. Pour in the diced tomatoes and tomato sauce, and add the basil. Simmer for about 20 minutes, stirring occasionally.
2. Meanwhile, bring a large pot of lightly salted water to a boil. Add penne pasta, and cook for 8 minutes, or until tender. Drain.
3. In a small bowl, whisk eggs with a fork. Place bread crumbs in a separate bowl. Stir the garlic powder, salt and pepper into the bread crumbs. Dip chicken cutlets into the egg, then press into the bread crumbs until completely coated.
4. Heat remaining olive oil in a large skillet over medium heat. Fry chicken for about 5 minutes per side, or until the coating is a nice dark brown color.
5. Remove chicken, and cut into slices. Toss the chicken slices into the sauce, and simmer for about 10 minutes. Stir in the cooked penne, simmer for a few more minutes to soak up the flavor, then serve.

BEST PEANUT BUTTER COOKIES EVER

Servings: 36 | Prep: 30m | Cooks: 10m | Total: 45m | Additional: 5m

NUTRITION FACTS

Calories: 132 | Carbohydrates: 13.9g | Fat: 7.5g | Protein: 3.9g | Cholesterol: 10mg

INGREDIENTS

- 2 cups peanut butter
- 2 teaspoons baking soda
- 2 cups white sugar
- 1 pinch salt
- 2 eggs
- 1 teaspoon vanilla extract

DIRECTIONS

1. Preheat oven to 350 degrees F (175 degrees C). Grease cookie sheets.
2. In a medium bowl, stir peanut butter and sugar together until smooth. Beat in the eggs, one at a time, then stir in the baking soda, salt, and vanilla. Roll dough into 1 inch balls and place them 2 inches apart onto the prepared cookie sheets. Press a criss-cross into the top using the back of a fork.
3. Bake for 8 to 10 minutes in the preheated oven. Allow cookies to cool on baking sheet for 5 minutes before removing to a wire rack to cool completely.

VEGAN BROWNIES

Servings: 16 | Prep: 15m | Cooks: 25m | Total: 50m | Additional: 10m

NUTRITION FACTS

Calories: 284 | Carbohydrates: 39.2g | Fat: 14.3g | Protein: 2.4g | Cholesterol: 0mg

INGREDIENTS

- 2 cups unbleached all-purpose flour
- 1 teaspoon salt
- 2 cups white sugar
- 1 cup water
- 3/4 cup unsweetened cocoa powder
- 1 cup vegetable oil
- 1 teaspoon baking powder
- 1 teaspoon vanilla extract

DIRECTIONS

1. Preheat the oven to 350 degrees F (175 degrees C).

2. In a large bowl, stir together the flour, sugar, cocoa powder, baking powder and salt. Pour in water, vegetable oil and vanilla; mix until well blended. Spread evenly in a 9x13 inch baking pan.

3. Bake for 25 to 30 minutes in the preheated oven, until the top is no longer shiny. Let cool for at least 10 minutes before cutting into squares.

MOLASSES SUGAR COOKIES

Servings: 72 | Prep: 25m | Cooks: 15m | Total: 3h40m | Additional: 3h

NUTRITION FACTS

Calories: 93 | Carbohydrates: 12.7g | Fat: 4.5g | Protein: 0.9g | Cholesterol: 5mg

INGREDIENTS

- 1 1/2 cups shortening
- 4 teaspoons baking soda
- 2 cups white sugar
- 2 teaspoons ground cinnamon
- 1/2 cup molasses
- 1 teaspoon ground cloves
- 2 eggs
- 1 teaspoon ground ginger
- 4 cups all-purpose flour
- 1 teaspoon salt

DIRECTIONS

1. Melt the shortening in a large pan on the stove, and cool.

2. Add sugar, eggs, and molasses, beat well.

3. In a separate bowl, sift dry ingredients together and add to the pan. Mix well and chill 3 hours or overnight.

4. Form into walnut-size balls. Roll in granulated sugar. Place on greased cookie sheet about 2 inches apart.

5. Bake at 375 degrees F (190 degrees C) for 8-10 minutes.

6. Store in an airtight container to keep from getting overly crisp. If they do lose their softness, an easy way to restore it is to place one slice of fresh bread in the container with the cookies for a couple of hours or overnight and they will be soft again!

MARINATED TUNA STEAK
Servings: 4 | Prep: 10m | Cooks: 11m | Total: 51m

NUTRITION FACTS
Calories: 200 | Carbohydrates: 3.7g | Fat: 7.9g | Protein: 27.4g | Cholesterol: 51mg

INGREDIENTS
- 1/4 cup orange juice
- 1 clove garlic, minced
- 1/4 cup soy sauce
- 1/2 teaspoon chopped fresh oregano
- 2 tablespoons olive oil
- 1/2 teaspoon ground black pepper
- 1 tablespoon lemon juice
- 4 (4 ounce) tuna steaks
- 2 tablespoons chopped fresh parsley

DIRECTIONS
1. In a large non-reactive dish, mix together the orange juice, soy sauce, olive oil, lemon juice, parsley, garlic, oregano, and pepper. Place the tuna steaks in the marinade and turn to coat. Cover, and refrigerate for at least 30 minutes.
2. Preheat grill for high heat.
3. Lightly oil grill grate. Cook the tuna steaks for 5 to 6 minutes, then turn and baste with the marinade. Cook for an additional 5 minutes, or to desired doneness. Discard any remaining marinade.

MOM'S GINGER SNAPS
Servings: 36 | Prep: 15m | Cooks: 12m | Total: 40m | Additional: 13m

NUTRITION FACTS
Calories: 105 | Carbohydrates: 15g | Fat: 4.8g | Protein: 0.9g | Cholesterol: 5mg

INGREDIENTS
- 1 cup packed brown sugar
- 1/4 teaspoon salt
- 3/4 cup vegetable oil
- 1/2 teaspoon ground cloves
- 1/4 cup molasses
- 1 teaspoon ground cinnamon
- 1 egg
- 1 teaspoon ground ginger

- 2 cups all-purpose flour
- 1/3 cup white sugar for decoration
- 2 teaspoons baking soda

DIRECTIONS

1. Preheat oven to 375 degrees F (190 degrees C).
2. In a large bowl, mix together the brown sugar, oil, molasses, and egg. Combine the flour, baking soda, salt, cloves, cinnamon, and ginger; stir into the molasses mixture. Roll dough into 1 1/4 inch balls. Roll each ball in white sugar before placing 2 inches apart on ungreased cookie sheets.
3. Bake for 10 to 12 minutes in preheated oven, or until center is firm. Cool on wire racks.

BROCCOLI BEEF

Servings: 4 | Prep: 15m | Cooks: 15m | Total: 30m

NUTRITION FACTS

Calories: 178 | Carbohydrates: 19g | Fat: 3.2g | Protein: 19.2g | Cholesterol: 39mg

INGREDIENTS

- 1/4 cup all-purpose flour
- 1 pound boneless round steak, cut into bite size pieces
- 1 (10.5 ounce) can beef broth
- 1/4 teaspoon chopped fresh ginger root
- 2 tablespoons white sugar
- 1 clove garlic, minced
- 2 tablespoons soy sauce
- 4 cups chopped fresh broccoli

DIRECTIONS

1. In a small bowl, combine flour, broth, sugar, and soy sauce. Stir until sugar and flour are dissolved.
2. In a large skillet or wok over high heat, cook and stir beef 2 to 4 minutes, or until browned. Stir in broth mixture, ginger, garlic, and broccoli. Bring to a boil, then reduce heat. Simmer 5 to 10 minutes, or until sauce thickens.

BISCOTTI

Servings: 15 | Prep: 25m | Cooks: 40m | Total: 40m

NUTRITION FACTS

Calories: 83 | Carbohydrates: 12.3g | Fat: 3.1g | Protein: 1.4g | Cholesterol: 013mg

INGREDIENTS

- 1/2 cup vegetable oil
- 3 eggs
- 1 cup white sugar
- 1 tablespoon baking powder
- 3 1/4 cups all-purpose flour
- 1 tablespoon anise extract, or 3 drops anise oil

DIRECTIONS

1. Preheat the oven to 375 degrees F (190 degrees C). Grease cookie sheets or line with parchment paper.
2. In a medium bowl, beat together the oil, eggs, sugar and anise flavoring until well blended. Combine the flour and baking powder, stir into the egg mixture to form a heavy dough. Divide dough into two pieces. Form each piece into a roll as long as your cookie sheet. Place roll onto the prepared cookie sheet, and press down to 1/2 inch thickness.
3. Bake for 25 to 30 minutes in the preheated oven, until golden brown. Remove from the baking sheet to cool on a wire rack. When The cookies are cool enough to handle, slice each one crosswise into 1/2 inch slices. Place the slices cut side up back onto the baking sheet. Bake for an additional 6 to 10 minutes on each side. Slices should be lightly toasted.

MOLASSES COOKIES

Servings: 30 | Prep: 10m | Cooks: 10m | Total: 1h20m | Additional: 1h

NUTRITION FACTS

Calories: 120 | Carbohydrates: 18.6g | Fat: 4.7g | Protein: 1.1g | Cholesterol: 6mg

INGREDIENTS

- 3/4 cup margarine, melted
- 1/2 teaspoon salt
- 1 cup white sugar
- 1 teaspoon ground cinnamon
- 1 egg
- 1/2 teaspoon ground cloves
- 1/4 cup molasses
- 1/2 teaspoon ground ginger
- 2 cups all-purpose flour
- 1/2 cup white sugar
- 2 teaspoons baking soda

DIRECTIONS

1. In a medium bowl, mix together the melted margarine, 1 cup sugar, and egg until smooth. Stir in the molasses. Combine the flour, baking soda, salt, cinnamon, cloves, and ginger; blend into the molasses mixture. Cover, and chill dough for 1 hour.
2. Preheat oven to 375 degrees F (190 degrees C). Roll dough into walnut sized balls, and roll them in the remaining white sugar. Place cookies 2 inches apart onto ungreased baking sheets.
3. Bake for 8 to 10 minutes in the preheated oven, until tops are cracked. Cool on wire racks.

PESTO PASTA WITH CHICKEN

Servings: 8 | Prep: 10m | Cooks: 20m | Total: 30m

NUTRITION FACTS

Calories: 328 | Carbohydrates: 43.3g | Fat: 10.1g | Protein: 17.4g | Cholesterol: 22mg

INGREDIENTS

- 1 (16 ounce) package bow tie pasta
- crushed red pepper flakes to taste
- 1 teaspoon olive oil
- 1/3 cup oil-packed sun-dried tomatoes, drained and cut into strips

- 2 cloves garlic, minced
- 1/2 cup pesto sauce
- 2 boneless skinless chicken breasts, cut into bite-size pieces

DIRECTIONS

1. Bring a large pot of lightly salted water to a boil. Add pasta and cook for 8 to 10 minutes or until al dente; drain.
2. Heat oil in a large skillet over medium heat. Saute garlic until tender, then stir in chicken. Season with red pepper flakes. Cook until chicken is golden, and cooked through.
3. In a large bowl, combine pasta, chicken, sun-dried tomatoes and pesto. Toss to coat evenly.

EASY GUACAMOLE

Servings: 16 | Prep: 10m | Cooks: 30m | Total: 40m

NUTRITION FACTS

Calories: 45 | Carbohydrates: 3.4g | Fat: 3.7g | Protein: 0.7g | Cholesterol: 0mg

INGREDIENTS

- 2 avocados
- 1 ripe tomato, chopped
- 1 small onion, finely chopped
- 1 lime, juiced
- 1 clove garlic, minced
- salt and pepper to taste

DIRECTIONS

1. Peel and mash avocados in a medium serving bowl. Stir in onion, garlic, tomato, lime juice, salt and pepper. Season with remaining lime juice and salt and pepper to taste. Chill for half an hour to blend flavors.

PUMPKIN CAKE

Servings: 14 | Prep: 30m | Cooks: 30m | Total: 1h

NUTRITION FACTS

Calories: 438 | Carbohydrates: 46.8g | Fat: 26.8g | Protein: 5.3g | Cholesterol: 53mg

INGREDIENTS

- 2 cups white sugar
- 3 teaspoons baking powder
- 1 1/4 cups vegetable oil
- 2 teaspoons baking soda
- 1 teaspoon vanilla extract
- 1/4 teaspoon salt
- 2 cups canned pumpkin
- 2 teaspoons ground cinnamon
- 4 eggs
- 1 cup chopped walnuts (optional
- 2 cups all-purpose flour

DIRECTIONS

1. Preheat oven to 350 degrees F (175 degrees C). Grease and flour a 12x18 inch pan. Sift together the flour, baking powder, baking soda, salt and cinnamon. Set aside.
2. In a large bowl combine sugar and oil. Blend in vanilla and pumpkin, then beat in eggs one at a time. Gradually beat in flour mixture. Stir in nuts. Spread batter into prepared 12x18 inch pan.
3. Bake in the preheated oven for 30 minutes, or until a toothpick inserted into the center of the cake comes out clean. Allow to cool.

CHILI-LIME CHICKEN KABOBS

Servings: 4 | Prep: 15m | Cooks: 10m | Total: 1h30m | Additional: 1h

NUTRITION FACTS

Calories: 227 | Carbohydrates: 3.2g | Fat: 13g | Protein: 23.9g | Cholesterol: 65mg

INGREDIENTS

- 3 tablespoons olive oil
- 1/2 teaspoon garlic powder
- 1 1/2 tablespoons red wine vinegar
- cayenne pepper to taste
- 1 lime, juiced
- salt and freshly ground black pepper to taste
- 1 teaspoon chili powder
- 1 pound skinless, boneless chicken breast halves - cut into 1 1/2 inch pieces
- 1/2 teaspoon paprika
- skewers
- 1/2 teaspoon onion powder

DIRECTIONS

1. In a small bowl, whisk together the olive oil, vinegar, and lime juice. Season with chili powder, paprika, onion powder, garlic powder, cayenne pepper, salt, and black pepper. Place the chicken in a shallow baking dish with the sauce, and stir to coat. Cover, and marinate in the refrigerator at least 1 hour.
2. Preheat the grill for medium-high heat. Thread chicken onto skewers, and discard marinade.
3. Lightly oil the grill grate. Grill skewers for 10 to 15 minutes, or until the chicken juices run clear.

CHEWY PEANUT BUTTER BROWNIES

Servings: 16 | Prep: 15m | Cooks: 25m | Total: 40m

NUTRITION FACTS

Calories: 177 | Carbohydrates: 22.8g | Fat: 8.5g | Protein: 3.7g | Cholesterol: 23mg

INGREDIENTS

- 1/2 cup peanut butter
- 1/2 teaspoon vanilla extract
- 1/3 cup margarine, softened
- 1 cup all-purpose flour
- 2/3 cup white sugar
- 1 teaspoon baking powder
- 1/2 cup packed brown sugar
- 1/4 teaspoon salt

- 2 egg

DIRECTIONS

1. Preheat oven to 350 degrees F (175 degrees C). Grease a 9x9 inch baking pan.
2. In a medium bowl, cream together peanut butter and margarine. Gradually blend in the brown sugar, white sugar, eggs, and vanilla; mix until fluffy. Combine flour, baking powder, and salt; stir into the peanut butter mixture until well blended.
3. Bake for 30 to 35 minutes in preheated oven, or until the top springs back when touched. Cool, and cut into 16 squares.

GRILLED BROWN SUGAR PORK CHOPS

Servings: 6 | Prep: 20m | Cooks: 20m | Total: 40m

NUTRITION FACTS

Calories: 262 | Carbohydrates: 21.5g | Fat: 13.7g | Protein: 13.3g | Cholesterol: 36mg

INGREDIENTS

- 1/2 cup brown sugar, firmly packed
- salt and pepper to taste
- 1/2 cup apple juice
- 2 teaspoons cornstarch
- 4 tablespoons vegetable oil
- 1/2 cup water
- 1 tablespoon soy sauce
- 6 boneless pork chops
- 1/2 teaspoon ground ginger

DIRECTIONS

1. Preheat an outdoor grill for high heat.
2. In a small saucepan, combine brown sugar, apple juice, oil, soy sauce, ginger, salt , and pepper. Bring to boil. Combine water and cornstarch in small bowl, and whisk into brown sugar mixture. Stir until thick.
3. Brush grate lightly with oil before placing pork chops on the grill. Cook over hot coals for 10 to 12 minutes, turning once. Brush with sauce just before removing chops from grill. Serve with remaining sauce.

SALMON WITH BROWN SUGAR GLAZE

Servings: 4 | Prep: 5m | Cooks: 10m | Total: 15m

NUTRITION FACTS

Calories: 330 | Carbohydrates: 15g | Fat: 16.2g | Protein: 29g | Cholesterol: 83mg

INGREDIENTS

- 1/4 cup packed light brown sugar
- 4 (6 ounce) boneless salmon fillets
- 2 tablespoons Dijon mustard
- salt and ground black pepper to taste

DIRECTIONS

1. Preheat the oven's broiler and set the oven rack at about 6 inches from the heat source; prepare the rack of a broiler pan with cooking spray.
2. Season the salmon with salt and pepper and arrange onto the prepared broiler pan. Whisk together the brown sugar and Dijon mustard in a small bowl; spoon mixture evenly onto top of salmon fillets.
3. Cook under the preheated broiler until the fish flakes easily with a fork, 10 to 15 minutes.

SNICKERDOODLES

Servings: 36 | Prep: 15m | Cooks: 10m | Total: 30m | Additional: 5m

NUTRITION FACTS

Calories: 125 | Carbohydrates: 16.5g | Fat: 6.1g | Protein: 1.3g | Cholesterol: 10mg

INGREDIENTS

- 1 cup shortening
- 2 teaspoons cream of tartar
- 1 1/2 cups white sugar
- 1/2 teaspoon salt
- 2 eggs
- 2 tablespoons white sugar
- 2 3/4 cups all-purpose flour
- 2 teaspoons ground cinnamon
- 1 teaspoon baking soda

DIRECTIONS

1. Preheat oven to 375 degrees F (190 degrees C).
2. In a medium bowl, cream together the shortening and 1 1/2 cups sugar. Stir in the eggs. Sift together the flour, baking soda, cream of tartar, and salt; stir into the creamed mixture until well blended. In a small bowl, stir together the 2 tablespoons of sugar, and the cinnamon. Roll dough into walnut sized balls, then roll the balls in the cinnamon-sugar. Place them onto an unprepared cookie sheet, two inches apart.
3. Bake for 8 to 10 minutes in the preheated oven. Edges should be slightly brown. Remove from sheets to cool on wire racks.

CHOCOLATE ZUCCHINI CAKE

Servings: 24 | Prep: 15m | Cooks: 50m | Total: 1h5m

NUTRITION FACTS

Calories: 269 | Carbohydrates: 27.2g | Fat: 17.5g | Protein: 3.4g | Cholesterol: 31mg

INGREDIENTS

- 2 cups all-purpose flour
- 1 teaspoon ground cinnamon
- 2 cups white sugar
- 4 eggs
- 3/4 cup unsweetened cocoa powder
- 1 1/2 cups vegetable oil
- 2 teaspoons baking soda
- 3 cups grated zucchini
- 1 teaspoon baking powder

- 3/4 cup chopped walnuts
- 1/2 teaspoon salt

DIRECTIONS

1. Preheat oven to 350 degrees F (175 degrees C). Grease and flour a 9x13 inch baking pan.
2. In a medium bowl, stir together the flour, sugar, cocoa, baking soda, baking powder, salt and cinnamon. Add the eggs and oil, mix well. Fold in the nuts and zucchini until they are evenly distributed. Pour into the prepared pan.
3. Bake for 50 to 60 minutes in the preheated oven, until a knife inserted into the center comes out clean. Cool cake completely before frosting with your favorite frosting.

FRIED CABBAGE

Servings: 6 | Prep: 20m | Cooks: 25m | Total: 45m

NUTRITION FACTS

Calories: 47 | Carbohydrates: 5.2g | Fat: 2g | Protein: 2.8g | Cholesterol: 5mg

INGREDIENTS

- 3 slices bacon, chopped
- 1 pinch white sugar
- 1/4 cup chopped onion
- salt and pepper to taste
- 6 cups cabbage, cut into thin wedges
- 1 tablespoon cider vinegar
- 2 tablespoons water

DIRECTIONS

1. Place bacon in a large, deep skillet. Cook over medium-high heat until evenly brown. Remove bacon, and set aside.
2. Cook onion in the hot bacon grease until tender. Add cabbage, and stir in water, sugar, salt, and pepper. Cook until cabbage wilts, about 15 minutes. Stir in bacon. Splash with vinegar before serving.

VEGAN CHOCOLATE CAKE

Servings: 8 | Prep: 15m | Cooks: 45m | Total: 1h

NUTRITION FACTS

Calories: 275 | Carbohydrates: 44.6g | Fat: 9.7g | Protein: 3g | Cholesterol: 0mg

INGREDIENTS

- 1 1/2 cups all-purpose flour
- 1/3 cup vegetable oil
- 1 cup white sugar
- 1 teaspoon vanilla extract
- 1/4 cup cocoa powder
- 1 teaspoon distilled white vinegar
- 1 teaspoon baking soda
- 1 cup water
- 1/2 teaspoon salt

DIRECTIONS

1. Preheat oven to 350 degrees F (175 degrees C). Lightly grease one 9x5 inch loaf pan.
2. Sift together the flour, sugar, cocoa, baking soda and salt. Add the oil, vanilla, vinegar and water. Mix together until smooth.
3. Pour into prepared pan and bake at 350 degrees F (175 degrees C) for 45 minutes. Remove from oven and allow to cool.

GRILLED TILAPIA WITH MANGO SALSA
Servings: 2 | Prep: 45m | Cooks: 10m | Total: 1h55m

NUTRITION FACTS
Calories: 634 | Carbohydrates: 33.4g | Fat: 40.2g | Protein: 36.3g | Cholesterol: 62mg

INGREDIENTS
- 1/3 cup extra-virgin olive oil
- 1 large ripe mango, peeled, pitted and diced
- 1 tablespoon lemon juice
- 1/2 red bell pepper, diced
- 1 tablespoon minced fresh parsley
- 2 tablespoons minced red onion
- 1 clove garlic, minced
- 1 tablespoon chopped fresh cilantro
- 1 teaspoon dried basil
- 1 jalapeno pepper, seeded and minced
- 1 teaspoon ground black pepper
- 2 tablespoons lime juice
- 1/2 teaspoon salt
- 1 tablespoon lemon juice
- 2 (6 ounce) tilapia fillets
- salt and pepper to taste

DIRECTIONS

1. Whisk together the extra-virgin olive oil, 1 tablespoon lemon juice, parsley, garlic, basil, 1 teaspoon pepper, and 1/2 teaspoon salt in a bowl and pour into a resealable plastic bag. Add the tilapia fillets, coat with the marinade, squeeze out excess air, and seal the bag. Marinate in the refrigerator for 1 hour.
2. Prepare the mango salsa by combining the mango, red bell pepper, red onion, cilantro, and jalapeno pepper in a bowl. Add the lime juice and 1 tablespoon of lemon juice, and toss well. Season to taste with salt and pepper, and refrigerate until ready to serve.
3. Preheat an outdoor grill for medium-high heat, and lightly oil grate.
4. Remove the tilapia from the marinade, and shake off excess. Discard the remaining marinade. Grill the fillets until the fish is no longer translucent in the center, and flakes easily with a fork, 3 to 4 minutes per side, depending on the thickness of the fillets. Serve the tilapia topped with mango salsa.

SLOW COOKER CHICKEN CACCIATORE
Servings: 6 | Prep: 15m | Cooks: 9h | Total: 9h15m

NUTRITION FACTS
Calories: 261 | Carbohydrates: 23.7g | Fat: 6.1g | Protein: 27.1g | Cholesterol: 63mg

INGREDIENTS
- 6 skinless, boneless chicken breast halves
- 8 ounces fresh mushrooms, sliced
- 1 (28 ounce) jar spaghetti sauce
- 1 onion, finely diced
- 2 green bell pepper, seeded and cubed
- 2 tablespoons minced garlic

DIRECTIONS
1. Put the chicken in the slow cooker. Top with the spaghetti sauce, green bell peppers, mushrooms, onion, and garlic.
2. Cover, and cook on Low for 7 to 9 hours.

FRENCH DIP SANDWICHES
Servings: 10 | Prep: 10m | Cooks: 12h | Total: 12h10m

NUTRITION FACTS
Calories: 372 | Carbohydrates: 29.8g | Fat: 14.4g | Protein: 29.6g | Cholesterol: 76mg

INGREDIENTS
- 1 (4 pound) boneless beef roast
- 1 teaspoon dried rosemary, crushed
- 1/2 cup soy sauce
- 1 teaspoon dried thyme
- 1 beef bouillon cube
- 1 teaspoon garlic powder
- 1 bay leaf
- 20 slices French bread
- 3 whole black peppercorns

DIRECTIONS
1. Remove and discard all visible fat from the roast. Place trimmed roast in a slow cooker.
2. In a medium bowl, combine soy sauce, bouillon, bay leaf, peppercorns, rosemary, thyme, and garlic powder. Pour mixture over roast, and add enough water to almost cover roast. Cover, and cook on Low heat for 10 to 12 hours, or until meat is very tender.
3. Remove meat from broth, reserving broth. Shred meat with a fork, and distribute on bread for sandwiches. Used reserved broth for dipping.

BLACK BEAN BROWNIES
Servings: 16 | Prep: 10m | Cooks: 30m | Total: 40m

NUTRITION FACTS
Calories: 126 | Carbohydrates: 18.1g | Fat: 5.3g | Protein: 3.3g | Cholesterol: 35mg

INGREDIENTS
- 1 (15.5 ounce) can black beans, rinsed and drained
- 1 teaspoon vanilla extract
- 3 eggs
- 3/4 cup white sugar
- 3 tablespoons vegetable oil

- 1 teaspoon instant coffee (optional)
- 1/4 cup cocoa powder
- 1/2 cup milk chocolate chips (optional)
- 1 pinch salt

DIRECTIONS

1. Preheat oven to 350 degrees F (175 degrees C). Lightly grease an 8x8 square baking dish.
2. Combine the black beans, eggs, oil, cocoa powder, salt, vanilla extract, sugar, and instant coffee in a blender; blend until smooth; pour the mixture into the prepared baking dish. Sprinkle the chocolate chips over the top of the mixture.
3. Bake in the preheated oven until the top is dry and the edges start to pull away from the sides of the pan, about 30 minutess.

GRILLED ASPARAGUS

Servings: 4 | Prep: 15m | Cooks: 3m | Total: 18m

NUTRITION FACTS

Calories: 53 | Carbohydrates: 4.4g | Fat: 3.5g | Protein: 2.5g | Cholesterol: 0mg

INGREDIENTS

- 1 pound fresh asparagus spears, trimmed
- salt and pepper to taste
- 1 tablespoon olive oil

DIRECTIONS

1. Preheat grill for high heat.
2. Lightly coat the asparagus spears with olive oil. Season with salt and pepper to taste.
3. Grill over high heat for 2 to 3 minutes, or to desired tenderness.

PINEAPPLE CHICKEN TENDERS

Servings: 10 | Prep: 30m | Cooks: 10m | Total: 1h10m | Additional: 30m

NUTRITION FACTS

Calories: 160 | Carbohydrates: 14.7g | Fat: 2.2g | Protein: 19.4g | Cholesterol: 52mg

INGREDIENTS

- 1 cup pineapple juice
- 2 pounds chicken breast tenderloins or strips
- 1/2 cup packed brown sugar
- skewers
- 1/3 cup light soy sauce

DIRECTIONS

1. In a small saucepan over medium heat, mix pineapple juice, brown sugar, and soy sauce. Remove from heat just before the mixture comes to a boil.
2. Place chicken tenders in a medium bowl. Cover with the pineapple marinade, and refrigerate for at least 30 minutes.
3. Preheat grill for medium heat. Thread chicken lengthwise onto wooden skewers.
4. Lightly oil the grill grate. Grill chicken tenders 5 minutes per side, or until juices run clear. They cook quickly, so watch them closely.

APPLE ENCHILADA DESSERT

Servings: 6 | Prep: 15m | Cooks: 20m | Total: 35m

NUTRITION FACTS

Calories: 484 | Carbohydrates: 88.3g | Fat: 13.5g | Protein: 4.5g | Cholesterol: 0mg

INGREDIENTS

- 1 (21 ounce) can apple pie filling
- 1/2 cup white sugar
- 6 (8 inch) flour tortillas
- 1/2 cup packed brown sugar
- 1 teaspoon ground cinnamon
- 1/2 cup water
- 1/3 cup margarine

DIRECTIONS

1. Preheat oven to 350 degrees F (175 degrees C).
2. Spoon fruit evenly onto all tortillas, sprinkle with cinnamon. Roll up tortillas and place seam side down on lightly greased 8x8 baking pan.
3. Bring margarine, sugars and water to a boil in a medium sauce pan. Reduce heat and simmer, stirring constantly for 3 minutes.
4. Pour sauce evenly over tortillas; sprinkle with extra cinnamon on top if desired. Bake in preheated oven for 20 minutes.
5. Makes 6 large tortillas; may be cut in half to serve 12.

PAT'S BAKED BEANS

Servings: 10 | Prep: 15m | Cooks: 1h15m | Total: 1h30m

NUTRITION FACTS

Calories: 399 | Carbohydrates: 68g | Fat: 9.1g | Protein: 14.1g | Cholesterol: 12mg

INGREDIENTS

- 6 slices bacon
- 1 (15 ounce) can garbanzo beans, drained
- 1 cup chopped onion
- 3/4 cup ketchup
- 1 clove garlic, minced
- 1/2 cup molasses
- 1 (16 ounce) can pinto beans
- 1/4 cup packed brown sugar
- 1 (16 ounce) can great Northern beans, drained
- 2 tablespoons Worcestershire sauce
- 1 (16 ounce) can baked beans
- 1 tablespoon yellow mustard
- 1 (16 ounce) can red kidney beans, drained
- 1/2 teaspoon pepper

DIRECTIONS

1. Preheat oven to 375 degrees F (190 degrees C).
2. Place bacon in a large, deep skillet. Cook over medium high heat until evenly brown. Drain, reserving 2 tablespoons of drippings, crumble and set aside in a large bowl. Cook the onion and

garlic in the reserved drippings until onion is tender; drain excess grease and transfer to the bowl with the bacon.

3. To the bacon and onions add pinto beans, northern beans, baked beans, kidney beans and garbanzo beans. Stir in ketchup, molasses, brown sugar, Worcestershire sauce, mustard and black pepper. Mix well and transfer to a 9x12 inch casserole dish.
4. Cover and bake in preheated oven for 1 hour.

GRILLED SHRIMP SCAMPI
Servings: 6 | Prep: 30m | Cooks: 6m | Total: 36m

NUTRITION FACTS
Calories: 173 | Carbohydrates: 1.6g | Fat: 10g | Protein: 18.7g | Cholesterol: 0mg

INGREDIENTS
- 1/4 cup olive oil
- ground black pepper to taste
- 1/4 cup lemon juice
- crushed red pepper flakes to taste (optional)
- 3 tablespoons chopped fresh parsley
- 1 1/2 pounds medium shrimp, peeled and deveined
- 1 tablespoon minced garlic

DIRECTIONS
1. In a large, non-reactive bowl, stir together the olive oil, lemon juice, parsley, garlic, and black pepper. Season with crushed red pepper, if desired. Add shrimp, and toss to coat. Marinate in the refrigerator for 30 minutes.
2. Preheat grill for high heat. Thread shrimp onto skewers, piercing once near the tail and once near the head. Discard any remaining marinade.
3. Lightly oil grill grate. Grill for 2 to 3 minutes per side, or until opaque.

BLUEBERRY CRUMB BARS
Servings: 15 | Prep: 15m | Cooks: 45m | Total: 1h

NUTRITION FACTS
Calories: 318 | Carbohydrates: 45.3g | Fat: 14.4g | Protein: 3.3g | Cholesterol: 12mg

INGREDIENTS
- 1 cup white sugar
- 1/4 teaspoon salt (optional)
- 1 teaspoon baking powder
- 1 pinch ground cinnamon (optional)
- 3 cups all-purpose flour
- 4 cups fresh blueberries
- 1 cup shortening
- 1/2 cup white sugar
- 1 egg
- 3 teaspoons cornstarch

DIRECTIONS
1. Preheat the oven to 375 degrees F (190 degrees C). Grease a 9x13 inch pan.

2. In a medium bowl, stir together 1 cup sugar, 3 cups flour, and baking powder. Mix in salt and cinnamon, if desired. Use a fork or pastry cutter to blend in the shortening and egg. Dough will be crumbly. Pat half of dough into the prepared pan.
3. In another bowl, stir together the sugar and cornstarch. Gently mix in the blueberries. Sprinkle the blueberry mixture evenly over the crust. Crumble remaining dough over the berry layer.
4. Bake in preheated oven for 45 minutes, or until top is slightly brown. Cool completely before cutting into squares.

SLOW COOKER ADOBO CHICKEN
Servings: 6 | Prep: 30m | Cooks: 8h | Total: 8h30m

NUTRITION FACTS
Calories: 254 | Carbohydrates: 5.3g | Fat: 14.7g | Protein: 23g | Cholesterol: 61mg

INGREDIENTS
- 1 small sweet onion, sliced
- 1/2 cup vinegar
- 8 cloves garlic, crushed
- 1 (3 pound) whole chicken, cut into pieces
- 3/4 cup low sodium soy sauce

DIRECTIONS
1. Place chicken in a slow cooker. In a small bowl mix the onion, garlic, soy sauce, and vinegar, and pour over the chicken. Cook on Low for 6 to 8 hours.

SLOW COOKED CORNED BEEF FOR SANDWICHES
Servings: 15 | Prep: 4h | Cooks: 4h | Total: 4h15m

NUTRITION FACTS
Calories: 229 | Carbohydrates: 4.2g | Fat: 15.1g | Protein: 15g | Cholesterol: 78mg

INGREDIENTS
- 2 (3 pound) corned beef briskets with spice packets
- 1/4 cup peppercorns
- 2 (12 fluid ounce) bottles beer
- 1 bulb garlic cloves, separated and peeled
- 2 bay leaves

DIRECTIONS
1. Place the corned beef briskets into a large pot. Sprinkle in one of the spice packets, and discard the other one or save for other uses. Pour in the beer, and fill the pot with enough water to cover the briskets by 1 inch. Add the bay leaves, peppercorns and garlic cloves. Cover, and bring to a boil.
2. Once the liquid comes to a boil, reduce the heat to medium-low, and simmer for 4 to 5 hours, checking hourly, and adding more water if necessary to keep the meat covered.
3. Carefully remove the meat from the pot, as it will be extremely tender. Set on a cutting board, and allow it to rest until it firms up a bit, about 10 minutes. Slice or shred to serve. I discard the cooking liquid, but it can be used to cook cabbage and other vegetables if desired.

SLOW COOKER CRANBERRY PORK

Servings: 6 | Prep: 10m | Cooks: 4h | Total: 4h10m

NUTRITION FACTS

Calories: 374 | Carbohydrates: 32.9g | Fat: 15.1g | Protein: 26.8g | Cholesterol: 80mg

INGREDIENTS

- 1 (16 ounce) can cranberry sauce
- 1 onion, sliced
- 1/3 cup French salad dressing
- 1 (3 pound) boneless pork loin roast

DIRECTIONS

1. In a medium bowl, stir together the cranberry sauce, salad dressing, and onion. Place pork in a slow cooker, and cover with the sauce mixture.
2. Cover, and cook on High for 4 hours, or on Low for 8 hours. Pork is done when the internal temperature has reached 145 degrees F (63 degrees C).

KATHY'S DELICIOUS WHOLE SLOW COOKER CHICKEN

Servings: 6 | Prep: 15m | Cooks: 8h | Total: 8h15m

NUTRITION FACTS

Calories: 393 | Carbohydrates: 14.3g | Fat: 27.6g | Protein: 22.1g | Cholesterol: 62mg

INGREDIENTS

- 1 (3 pound) whole chicken, skin removed
- 1 teaspoon Worcestershire sauce
- 1/2 cup chicken broth
- 2 teaspoons balsamic vinegar
- 1/3 cup soy sauce
- 2 teaspoons lemon juice
- 1/3 cup olive oil
- 1 teaspoon sesame oil
- 1/4 cup honey
- 2 tablespoons minced garlic

DIRECTIONS

1. Remove skin from chicken, and empty inner cavity of contents within. Pat chicken dry with a paper towel, and place inside the slow cooker.
2. In a bowl, stir together the chicken broth, soy sauce, olive oil, honey, Worcestershire sauce, balsamic vinegar, lemon juice, sesame oil, and minced garlic. Pour mixture over chicken, and cover.
3. Cook chicken on low setting for 8 hours, or 4 hours on high setting.

SESAME NOODLES

Servings: 8 | Prep: 15m | Cooks: 15m | Total: 30m

NUTRITION FACTS

Calories: 88 | Carbohydrates: 19.6g | Fat: 14.8g | Protein: 7.9g | Cholesterol: 0mg

INGREDIENTS

- 1 (16 ounce) package linguine pasta

- 6 tablespoons soy sauce
- 6 cloves garlic, minced
- 2 tablespoons sesame oil
- 6 tablespoons sugar
- 2 teaspoons chili sauce
- 6 tablespoons safflower oil
- 6 green onions, sliced
- 6 tablespoons rice vinegar
- 1 teaspoon sesame seeds, toasted

DIRECTIONS

1. Bring a pot of lightly salted water to boil. Add pasta, and cook until al dente, about 8 to 10 minutes. Drain, and transfer to a serving bowl.
2. Meanwhile, place a saucepan over medium-high heat. Stir in garlic, sugar, oil, vinegar, soy sauce, sesame oil, and chili sauce. Bring to a boil, stirring constantly, until sugar dissolves. Pour sauce over linguine, and toss to coat. Garnish with green onions and sesame seeds.

SLOW COOKER SPICY BLACK-EYED PEAS
Servings: 10 | Prep: 30m | Cooks: 6h | Total: 6h30m

NUTRITION FACTS
Calories: 199 | Carbohydrates: 30.2g | Fat: 2.9g | Protein: 14.1g | Cholesterol: 10mg

INGREDIENTS

- 6 cups water
- 8 ounces diced ham
- 1 cube chicken bouillon
- 4 slices bacon, chopped
- 1 pound dried black-eyed peas, sorted and rinsed
- 1/2 teaspoon cayenne pepper
- 1 onion, diced
- 1 1/2 teaspoons cumin
- 2 cloves garlic, diced
- salt, to taste
- 1 red bell pepper, stemmed, seeded, and diced
- 1 teaspoon ground black pepper
- 1 jalapeno chile, seeded and minced

DIRECTIONS

1. Pour the water into a slow cooker, add the bouillon cube, and stir to dissolve. Combine the black-eyed peas, onion, garlic, bell pepper, jalapeno pepper, ham, bacon, cayenne pepper, cumin, salt, and pepper; stir to blend. Cover the slow cooker and cook on Low for 6 to 8 hours until the beans are tender.

THE BEST SWEET AND SOUR MEATBALLS
Servings: 4 | Prep: 20m | Cooks: 30m | Total: 1h

NUTRITION FACTS

Calories: 516 | Carbohydrates: 67.1g | Fat: 16.8g | Protein: 24.5g | Cholesterol: 122mg

INGREDIENTS

- 1 pound ground beef
- 3 tablespoons all-purpose flour
- 1 egg
- 1 1/2 cups water
- 1/4 cup dry bread crumbs
- 1/4 cup distilled white vinegar
- 1 onion, diced
- 3 tablespoons soy sauce
- 1 cup packed brown sugar

DIRECTIONS

1. In a medium bowl, combine the ground beef, egg, bread crumbs and onion. Mix thoroughly and shape into golf ball-sized balls.
2. In a large skillet over medium heat, gently brown the meatballs and set aside.
3. In a large saucepan, combine the brown sugar, flour, water, white vinegar and soy sauce. Mix thoroughly. Add meatballs and bring to a boil. Reduce heat and simmer, stirring often, for 30 minutes.

EASY MARINATED PORK TENDERLOIN

Servings: 3 | Prep: 10m | Cooks: 45m | Total: 1h55m | Additional: 1h

NUTRITION FACTS

Calories: 485 | Carbohydrates: 9g | Fat: 24.7g | Protein: 55.5g | Cholesterol: 169mg

INGREDIENTS

- 1/4 cup olive oil
- 3 tablespoons dijon honey mustard
- 1/4 cup soy sauce
- salt and ground black pepper to taste
- 1 clove garlic, minced
- 2 pounds pork tenderloin

DIRECTIONS

1. Whisk together the olive oil, soy sauce, garlic, mustard, salt, and pepper in a bowl. Place the pork loin in a large resealable plastic bag and pour in the marinade. Marinate in the refrigerator at least 1 hour before cooking.
2. Preheat an oven to 350 degrees F (175 degrees C).
3. Transfer the pork loin to a baking dish; pour marinade over the pork.
4. Cook in the preheated oven until the pork is no longer pink in the center, 45 to 60 minutes. An instant-read thermometer inserted into the center should read 145 degrees F (63 degrees C).

SEARED AHI TUNA STEAKS

Servings: 2 | Prep: 5m | Cooks: 12m | Total: 17m

NUTRITION FACTS

Calories: 301 | Carbohydrates: 0.7g | Fat: 17.8g | Protein: 33.3g | Cholesterol: 71mg

INGREDIENTS

- 2 (5 ounce) ahi tuna steaks
- 1/2 tablespoon butter
- 1 teaspoon kosher salt
- 2 tablespoons olive oil
- 1/4 teaspoon cayenne pepper
- 1 teaspoon whole peppercorns

DIRECTIONS

1. Season the tuna steaks with salt and cayenne pepper.
2. Melt the butter with the olive oil in a skillet over medium-high heat. Cook the peppercorns in the mixture until they soften and pop, about 5 minutes. Gently place the seasoned tuna in the skillet and cook to desired doneness, 1 1/2 minutes per side for rare.

BREAKFAST SAUSAGE

Servings: 6 | Prep: 10m | Cooks: 15m | Total: 25m

NUTRITION FACTS

Calories: 409 | Carbohydrates: 2.7g | Fat: 32.2g | Protein: 25.6g | Cholesterol: 109mg

INGREDIENTS

- 2 teaspoons dried sage
- 1 tablespoon brown sugar
- 2 teaspoons salt
- 1/8 teaspoon crushed red pepper flakes
- 1 teaspoon ground black pepper
- 1 pinch ground cloves
- 1/4 teaspoon dried marjoram
- 2 pounds ground pork

DIRECTIONS

1. In a small, bowl, combine the sage, salt, ground black pepper, marjoram, brown sugar, crushed red pepper and cloves. Mix well.
2. Place the pork in a large bowl and add the mixed spices to it. Mix well with your hands and form into patties.
3. Saute the patties in a large skillet over medium high heat for 5 minutes per side, or until internal pork temperature reaches 160 degrees F (73 degrees C).

SLOW COOKER BARBEQUE

Servings: 8 | Prep: 10m | Cooks: 9h | Total: 9h10m

NUTRITION FACTS

Calories: 343 | Carbohydrates: 23.3g | Fat: 17.9g | Protein: 20.5g | Cholesterol: 74mg

INGREDIENTS

- 1 (3 pound) boneless chuck roast
- salt and pepper to taste
- 1 teaspoon garlic powder
- 1 (18 ounce) bottle barbeque sauce
- 1 teaspoon onion powder

DIRECTIONS

1. Place roast into slow cooker. Sprinkle with garlic powder and onion powder, and season with salt and pepper. Pour barbeque sauce over meat. Cook on Low for 6 to 8 hours.
2. Remove meat from slow cooker, shred, and return to slow cooker. Cook for 1 more hour. Serve hot.

FRESH TOMATO SALSA

Servings: 4 | Prep: 10m | Cooks: 1h | Total: 1h10m

NUTRITION FACTS

Calories: 51 | Carbohydrates: 9.7g | Fat: 1.3g | Protein: 2.1g | Cholesterol: 0mg

INGREDIENTS

- 3 tomatoes, chopped
- 1/2 cup chopped fresh cilantro
- 1/2 cup finely diced onion
- 1 teaspoon salt
- 5 serrano chiles, finely chopped
- 2 teaspoons lime juice

DIRECTIONS

1. In a medium bowl, stir together tomatoes, onion, chili peppers, cilantro, salt, and lime juice. Chill for one hour in the refrigerator before serving.

CINNAMON-ROASTED ALMONDS

Servings: 4 | Prep: 15m | Cooks: 10m | Total: 45m

NUTRITION FACTS

Calories: 231 | Carbohydrates: 13.3g | Fat: 18g | Protein: 7.8g | Cholesterol: 0mg

INGREDIENTS

- 1 egg white
- 1/2 cup white sugar
- 1 teaspoon cold water
- 1/4 teaspoon salt
- 4 cups whole almonds
- 1/2 teaspoon ground cinnamon

DIRECTIONS

1. Preheat oven to 250 degrees F (120 degrees C). Lightly grease a 10x15 inch jellyroll pan.
2. Lightly beat the egg white; add water, and beat until frothy but not stiff. Add the nuts, and stir until well coated. Mix the sugar, salt, and cinnamon, and sprinkle over the nuts. Toss to coat, and spread evenly on the prepared pan.
3. Bake for 1 hour in the preheated oven, stirring occasionally, until golden. Allow to cool, then store nuts in airtight containers.

JAY'S JERK CHICKEN

Servings: 4 | Prep: 15m | Cooks: 30m | Total: 4h45m

NUTRITION FACTS

Calories: 385 | Carbohydrates: 15.4g | Fat: 18.2g | Protein: 39.2g | Cholesterol: 97mg

INGREDIENTS

- 6 green onions, chopped
- 2 tablespoons brown sugar
- 1 onion, chopped
- 1 tablespoon chopped fresh thyme
- 1 jalapeno pepper, seeded and minced
- 1/2 teaspoon ground cloves
- 3/4 cup soy sauce
- 1/2 teaspoon ground nutmeg
- 1/2 cup distilled white vinegar
- 1/2 teaspoon ground allspice
- 1/4 cup vegetable oil
- 1 1/2 pounds skinless, boneless chicken breast halves

DIRECTIONS

1. In a food processor or blender, combine the green onions, onion, jalapeno pepper, soy sauce, vinegar, vegetable oil, brown sugar, thyme, cloves, nutmeg and allspice. Mix for about 15 seconds.
2. Place the chicken in a medium bowl, and coat with the marinade. Refrigerate for 4 to 6 hours, or overnight.
3. Preheat grill for high heat.
4. Lightly oil grill grate. Cook chicken on the prepared grill 6 to 8 minutes, until juices run clear.

ROASTED LEMON HERB CHICKEN
Servings: 8 | Prep: 15m | Cooks: 1h30m | Total: 1h45m

NUTRITION FACTS

Calories: 405 | Carbohydrates: 3.6g | Fat: 29.2g | Protein: 32.2g | Cholesterol: 128mg

INGREDIENTS

- 2 teaspoons Italian seasoning
- 1/2 teaspoon ground black pepper
- 1/2 teaspoon seasoning salt
- 1 (3 pound) whole chicken
- 1/2 teaspoon mustard powder
- 2 lemons
- 1 teaspoon garlic powder
- 2 tablespoons olive oil

DIRECTIONS

1. Preheat oven to 350 degrees F (175 degrees C).
2. Combine the seasoning, salt, mustard powder, garlic powder and black pepper; set aside. Rinse the chicken thoroughly, and remove the giblets. Place chicken in a 9x13 inch baking dish. Sprinkle 1 1/2 teaspoons of the spice mixture inside the chicken. Rub the remaining mixture on the outside of the chicken.
3. Squeeze the juice of the 2 lemons into a small bowl or cup, and mix with the olive oil. Drizzle this oil/juice mixture over the chicken.
4. Bake in the preheated oven for 1 1/2 hours, or until juices run clear, basting several times with the remaining oil mixture.

ROAST LEG OF LAMB WITH ROSEMARY

Servings: 10 | Prep: 15m | Cooks: 1h20m | Total: 1d 1h35m

NUTRITION FACTS

Calories: 553 | Carbohydrates: 8.1g | Fat: 38.7g | Protein: 40.7g | Cholesterol: 156mg

INGREDIENTS

- 1/4 cup honey
- 1 teaspoon lemon zest
- 2 tablespoons prepared Dijon-style mustard
- 3 cloves garlic, minced
- 2 tablespoons chopped fresh rosemary
- 5 pounds whole leg of lamb
- 1 teaspoon freshly ground black pepper
- 1 teaspoon coarse sea salt

DIRECTIONS

1. In a small bowl, combine the honey, mustard, rosemary, ground black pepper, lemon zest and garlic. Mix well and apply to the lamb. Cover and marinate in the refrigerator overnight.
2. Preheat oven to 450 degrees F (230 degrees C).
3. Place lamb on a rack in a roasting pan and sprinkle with salt to taste.
4. Bake at 450 degrees F (230 degrees C) for 20 minutes, then reduce heat to 400 degrees F (200 degrees C) and roast for 55 to 60 more minutes for medium rare. The internal temperature should be at least 145 degrees F (63 degrees C) when taken with a meat thermometer. Let the roast rest for about 10 minutes before carving.

BAKED SWEET POTATOES

Servings: 4 | Prep: 10m | Cooks: 1h5m | Total: 1h15m

NUTRITION FACTS

Calories: 321 | Carbohydrates: 61g | Fat: 7.3g | Protein: 4.8g | Cholesterol: 0mg

INGREDIENTS

- 2 tablespoons olive oil
- 2 pinches salt
- 3 large sweet potatoes
- 2 pinches ground black pepper
- 2 pinches dried oregan

DIRECTIONS

1. Preheat oven to 350 degrees F (175 degrees C). Coat the bottom of a glass or non-stick baking dish with olive oil, just enough to coat.
2. Wash and peel the sweet potatoes. Cut them into medium size pieces. Place the cut sweet potatoes in the baking dish and turn them so that they are coated with the olive oil. Sprinkle moderately with oregano, and salt and pepper (to taste).
3. Bake in a preheated 350 degrees F (175 degrees C) oven for 60 minutes or until soft.

PRIZE WINNING BABY BACK RIBS

Servings: 6 | Prep: 30m | Cooks: 1h5m | Total: 1h35m

NUTRITION FACTS

Calories: 441 | Carbohydrates: 16.9g | Fat: 30g | Protein: 24.6g | Cholesterol: 117mg

INGREDIENTS

- 1 tablespoon ground cumin
- salt and pepper to taste
- 1 tablespoon chili powder
- 3 pounds baby back pork ribs
- 1 tablespoon paprika
- 1 cup barbeque sauce

DIRECTIONS

1. Preheat a gas grill for high heat, or arrange charcoal briquettes on one side of the barbeque. Lightly oil the grate.
2. In a small jar, combine cumin, chili powder, paprika, salt, and pepper. Close the lid, and shake to mix.
3. Trim the membrane sheath from the back of each rack. Run a small, sharp knife between the membrane and each rib, and snip off the membrane as much as possible. Sprinkle as much of the rub onto both sides of the ribs as desired. To prevent the ribs from becoming too dark and spicy, do not thoroughly rub the spices into the ribs. Store the unused portion of the spice mix for future use.
4. Place aluminum foil on lower rack to capture drippings and prevent flare-ups. Lay the ribs on the top rack of the grill (away from the coals, if you're using briquettes). Reduce gas heat to low, close lid, and leave undisturbed for 1 hour. Do not lift the lid at all.
5. Brush ribs with barbecue sauce, and grill an additional 5 minutes. Serve ribs as whole rack, or cut between each rib bone and pile individually on a platter.

SLOW COOKER LATIN CHICKEN

Servings: 6 | Prep: 25m | Cooks: 4h10m | Total: 4h35m

NUTRITION FACTS

Calories: 591 | Carbohydrates: 56.9g | Fat: 18.1g | Protein: 50.2g | Cholesterol: 137mg

INGREDIENTS

- 1 tablespoon olive oil
- 1/2 cup chicken broth
- 3 pounds skinless chicken thighs
- 1/4 cup loosely packed cilantro leaves
- salt and ground black pepper to taste
- 1 cup hot salsa
- 1/4 cup loosely packed cilantro leaves
- 2 teaspoons ground cumin
- 2 large sweet potatoes, cut into chunks
- 1/2 teaspoon ground allspice
- 1 red bell pepper, cut into strips
- 3 large cloves garlic, chopped
- 2 (15.5 ounce) cans black beans, rinsed and drained
- lime wedges, for garnish

DIRECTIONS

1. Heat the olive oil in a large skillet; season the chicken thighs with salt and pepper. Sprinkle 1/4 cup cilantro over the chicken thighs; brown the chicken in the frying pan, 3 to 5 minutes each side.
2. Arrange the chicken in the bottom of a slow cooker. Place the sweet potatoes, red bell pepper, and black beans on top of the chicken. Mix together the chicken broth, 1/4 cup cilantro leaves, salsa, cumin, allspice, and garlic together in a bowl; pour into the slow cooker. Set slow cooker to LOW and cook for 4 hours. Garnish with lime wedges to serve.

CHICKPEA CURRY

Servings: 8 | Prep: 10m | Cooks: 30m | Total: 40m

NUTRITION FACTS

Calories: 135 | Carbohydrates: 20.5g | Fat: 4.5g | Protein: 4.1g | Cholesterol: 0mg

INGREDIENTS

- 2 tablespoons vegetable oil
- 1 teaspoon ground coriander
- 2 onions, minced
- salt
- 2 cloves garlic, minced
- 1 teaspoon cayenne pepper
- 2 teaspoons fresh ginger root, finely chopped
- 1 teaspoon ground turmeric
- 6 whole cloves
- 2 (15 ounce) cans garbanzo beans
- 2 (2 inch) sticks cinnamon, crushed
- 1 cup chopped fresh cilantro
- 1 teaspoon ground cumin

DIRECTIONS

1. Heat oil in a large frying pan over medium heat, and fry onions until tender.
2. Stir in garlic, ginger, cloves, cinnamon, cumin, coriander, salt, cayenne, and turmeric. Cook for 1 minute over medium heat, stirring constantly. Mix in garbanzo beans and their liquid. Continue to cook and stir until all ingredients are well blended and heated through. Remove from heat. Stir in cilantro just before serving, reserving 1 tablespoon for garnish.

FISH FILLETS ITALIANO

Servings: 4 | Prep: 10m | Cooks: 15m | Total: 25m

NUTRITION FACTS

Calories: 230 | Carbohydrates: 8.2g | Fat: 9.4g | Protein: 21.2g | Cholesterol: 41mg

INGREDIENTS

- 2 tablespoons olive oil
- 1/2 cup black olives, pitted and sliced
- 1 onion, thinly sliced
- 1 tablespoon chopped fresh parsley
- 2 cloves garlic, minced
- 1/2 cup dry white wine

- 1 (14.5 ounce) can diced tomatoes
- 1 pound cod fillets

DIRECTIONS

1. In a large frying pan, heat oil over medium heat. Saute onions and garlic in olive oil until softened.
2. Stir in tomatoes, olives, parsley, and wine. Simmer for 5 minutes.
3. Place fillets in sauce. Simmer for about 5 more minutes, or until fish turns white.

SLOW COOKER ROAST BEEF

Servings: 6 | Prep: 5m | Cooks: 22h | Total: 22h5m

NUTRITION FACTS

Calories: 555 | Carbohydrates: 4.4g | Fat: 40.8g | Protein: 40.4g | Cholesterol: 161mg

INGREDIENTS

- 1/3 cup soy sauce
- 3 pounds beef chuck roast
- 1 (1 ounce) package dry onion soup mix
- 2 teaspoons freshly ground black pepper

DIRECTIONS

1. Pour soy sauce and dry onion soup mix into the slow cooker; mix well. Place chuck roast into the slow cooker. Add water until the top 1/2 inch of the roast is not covered. Sprinkle ground pepper on top.
2. Cover and cook on low for 22 hours.

SPICY CHICKEN BREASTS

Servings: 4 | Prep: 15m | Cooks: 15m | Total: 30m

NUTRITION FACTS

Calories: 173 | Carbohydrates: 9.2g | Fat: 2.4g | Protein: 29.2g | Cholesterol: 68mg

INGREDIENTS

- 2 1/2 tablespoons paprika
- 1 tablespoon dried thyme
- 2 tablespoons garlic powder
- 1 tablespoon ground cayenne pepper
- 1 tablespoon salt
- 1 tablespoon ground black pepper
- 1 tablespoon onion powder
- 4 skinless, boneless chicken breast halves

DIRECTIONS

1. In a medium bowl, mix together the paprika, garlic powder, salt, onion powder, thyme, cayenne pepper, and ground black pepper. Set aside about 3 tablespoons of this seasoning mixture for the chicken; store the remainder in an airtight container for later use (for seasoning fish, meats, or vegetables).
2. Preheat grill for medium-high heat. Rub some of the reserved 3 tablespoons of seasoning onto both sides of the chicken breasts.
3. Lightly oil the grill grate. Place chicken on the grill, and cook for 6 to 8 minutes on each side, until juices run clear.

GINGER VEGGIE STIR-FRY

Servings: 6 | Prep: 25m | Cooks: 15m | Total: 40m

NUTRITION FACTS

Calories: 119 | Carbohydrates: 8g | Fat: 9.3g | Protein: 2.2g | Cholesterol: 0mg

INGREDIENTS

- 1 tablespoon cornstarch
- 3/4 cup julienned carrots
- 1 1/2 cloves garlic, crushed
- 1/2 cup halved green beans
- 2 teaspoons chopped fresh ginger root, divided
- 2 tablespoons soy sauce
- 1/4 cup vegetable oil, divided
- 2 1/2 tablespoons water
- 1 small head broccoli, cut into florets
- 1/4 cup chopped onion
- 1/2 cup snow peas
- 1/2 tablespoon salt

DIRECTIONS

1. In a large bowl, blend cornstarch, garlic, 1 teaspoon ginger, and 2 tablespoons vegetable oil until cornstarch is dissolved. Mix in broccoli, snow peas, carrots, and green beans, tossing to lightly coat.
2. Heat remaining 2 tablespoons oil in a large skillet or wok over medium heat. Cook vegetables in oil for 2 minutes, stirring constantly to prevent burning. Stir in soy sauce and water. Mix in onion, salt, and remaining 1 teaspoon ginger. Cook until vegetables are tender but still crisp.

BAKED BEANS

Servings: 6 | Prep: 20m | Cooks: 1h | Total: 1h20m

NUTRITION FACTS

Calories: 287 | Carbohydrates: 52.3g | Fat: 6.5g | Protein: 8.9g | Cholesterol: 16mg

INGREDIENTS

- 2 (15 ounce) cans baked beans with pork
- 1 teaspoon Worcestershire sauce
- 1/2 cup packed brown sugar
- 1 teaspoon red wine vinegar
- 1/2 onion, chopped
- salt and pepper to taste
- 1/2 cup ketchup
- 2 slices bacon
- 1 tablespoon prepared mustard

DIRECTIONS

1. Preheat oven to 350 degrees F (175 degrees C).
2. In a 9x9 inch baking dish, combine the pork and beans, brown sugar, onion, ketchup, mustard, Worcestershire sauce and vinegar and season with salt and pepper to taste. Top with the bacon slices.
3. Bake at 350 degrees F (175 degrees C) for 1 hour, or until sauce is thickened and bacon is cooked.

BEST GUACAMOLE

Servings: 16 | Prep: 5m | Cooks: 1h | Total: 1h5m

NUTRITION FACTS

Calories: 56 | Carbohydrates: 2.6g | Fat: 5.4g | Protein: 0.6g | Cholesterol: 0mg

INGREDIENTS

- 2 avocados
- 1/2 teaspoon salt
- 1/2 lemon, juiced
- 2 tablespoons olive oil
- 2 tablespoons chopped onion

DIRECTIONS

1. Cut the avocados into halves. Remove the seeds, and scoop out the pulp into a small bowl. Use a fork to mash the avocado. Stir in lemon juice, onion, salt, and olive oil. Cover the bowl, and refrigerate for 1 hour before serving.

PEPPERMINT MERINGUES

Servings: 48 | Prep: 20m | Cooks: 1h30m | Total: 5h | Additional: 3h10m

NUTRITION FACTS

Calories: 13 | Carbohydrates: 3.2g | Fat: 0g | Protein: 0.2g | Cholesterol: 0mg

INGREDIENTS

- 2 egg whites
- 1/2 cup white sugar
- 1/8 teaspoon salt
- 2 peppermint candy canes, crushed
- 1/8 teaspoon cream of tartar

DIRECTIONS

1. Preheat oven to 225 degrees F (110 degrees C). Line 2 cookie sheets with foil.
2. In a large glass or metal mixing bowl, beat egg whites, salt, and cream of tartar to soft peaks. Gradually add sugar, continuing to beat until whites form stiff peaks. Drop by spoonfuls 1 inch apart on the prepared cookie sheets. Sprinkle crushed peppermint candy over the cookies.
3. Bake for 1 1/2 hours in preheated oven. Meringues should be completely dry on the inside. Do not allow them to brown. Turn off oven. Keep oven door ajar, and let meringues sit in the oven until completely cool. Loosen from foil with metal spatula. Store loosely covered in cool dry place for up to 2 months.

SESAME GREEN BEANS

Servings: 4 | Prep: 5m | Cooks: 25m | Total: 30m

NUTRITION FACTS

Calories: 78 | Carbohydrates: 8.6g | Fat: 4.6g | Protein: 2.5g | Cholesterol: 0mg

INGREDIENTS

- 1 tablespoon olive oil
- 1/4 cup chicken broth
- 1 tablespoon sesame seeds

- 1/4 teaspoon salt
- 1 pound fresh green beans, cut into 2 inch pieces
- freshly ground black pepper to taste

DIRECTIONS

1. Heat oil in a large skillet or wok over medium heat. Add sesame seeds. When seeds start to darken, stir in green beans. Cook, stirring, until the beans turn bright green.
2. Pour in chicken broth, salt and pepper. Cover and cook until beans are tender-crisp, about 10 minutes. Uncover and cook until liquid evaporates.

EASY HERB ROASTED TURKEY

Servings: 16 | Prep: 15m | Cooks: 3h30m | Total: 4h15m

NUTRITION FACTS

Calories: 597 | Carbohydrates: 0.9g | Fat: 33.7g | Protein: 68.2g | Cholesterol: 198mg

INGREDIENTS

- 1 (12 pound) whole turkey
- 1 teaspoon ground sage
- 3/4 cup olive oil
- 1 teaspoon salt
- 2 tablespoons garlic powder
- 1/2 teaspoon black pepper
- 2 teaspoons dried basil
- 2 cups water

DIRECTIONS

1. Preheat oven to 325 degrees F (165 degrees C). Clean turkey (discard giblets and organs), and place in a roasting pan with a lid.
2. In a small bowl, combine olive oil, garlic powder, dried basil, ground sage, salt, and black pepper. Using a basting brush, apply the mixture to the outside of the uncooked turkey. Pour water into the bottom of the roasting pan, and cover.
3. Bake for 3 to 3 1/2 hours, or until the internal temperature of the thickest part of the thigh measures 180 degrees F (82 degrees C). Remove bird from oven, and allow to stand for about 30 minutes before carving.

ROAST PORK WITH MAPLE AND MUSTARD GLAZE

Servings: 8 | Prep: 15m | Cooks: 1h | Total: 1h25m | Additional: 10m

NUTRITION FACTS

Calories: 290 | Carbohydrates: 28.4g | Fat: 8.2g | Protein: 24.4g | Cholesterol: 68mg

INGREDIENTS

- 2 1/2 pounds boneless pork loin roast
- 2 1/2 tablespoons soy sauce
- 1 cup real maple syrup
- salt to taste
- 4 tablespoons prepared Dijon-style mustard
- ground black pepper to taste
- 2 1/2 tablespoons cider vinegar

DIRECTIONS

1. Preheat the oven to 350 degrees F (175 degrees C).
2. Stir together the maple syrup, mustard, vinegar, soy sauce, salt, and pepper in a small bowl. Place pork roast in a shallow roasting pan. Spread glaze evenly over pork roast.
3. Roast pork in the preheated oven uncovered, until internal temperature measured with a meat thermometer reaches 145 degrees F (63 degrees C), about 1 hour. Remove from oven, and let rest about 10 minutes before slicing to serve.

BEST BEEF DIP EVER

Servings: 10 | Prep: 10m | Cooks: 6h | Total: 6h10m

NUTRITION FACTS

Calories: 290 | Carbohydrates: 2.5g | Fat: 20.4g | Protein: 22.8g | Cholesterol: 82mg

INGREDIENTS

- 4 pounds beef chuck roast
- 3 bay leaves
- 1 tablespoon minced garlic
- 1 cup soy sauce
- 1 tablespoon dried rosemary
- 6 cups water

DIRECTIONS

1. Place roast in slow cooker. Season with garlic and rosemary and add bay leaves. Pour in soy sauce and water. Cook on Low setting for 6 to 10 hours. Unlike most roasts, the longer it cooks, the better.

VICKI'S HUSH PUPPIES

Servings: 8 | Prep: 10m | Cooks: 30m | Total: 40m

NUTRITION FACTS

Calories: 277 | Carbohydrates: 36.7g | Fat: 12.9g | Protein: 4.6g | Cholesterol: 46mg

INGREDIENTS

- 2 eggs, beaten
- 1 cup self-rising flour
- 1/2 cup white sugar
- 1 cup self-rising cornmeal
- 1 large onion, diced
- 1 quart oil for frying

DIRECTIONS

1. In a medium bowl, mix together eggs, sugar, and onion. Blend in flour and cornmeal.
2. Heat 2 inches of oil to 365 degrees F (185 degrees C). Drop batter by rounded teaspoonfuls in hot oil, and fry until golden brown. Cook in small batches to maintain oil temperature. Drain briefly on paper towels. Serve hot.

HOUSE FRIED RICE

Servings: 8 | Prep: 10m | Cooks: 30m | Total: 40m

Calories: 236 | Carbohydrates: 26.4g | Fat: 8.4g | Protein: 13g | Cholesterol: 59mg

INGREDIENTS

- 1 1/2 cups uncooked white rice
- 2 stalks celery, chopped
- 3 tablespoons sesame oil
- 2 carrots - peeled and diced
- 1 small onion, chopped
- 1 green bell pepper, chopped
- 1 clove garlic, chopped
- 1/2 cup green peas
- 1 cup small shrimp - peeled and deveined
- 1 egg, beaten
- 1/2 cup diced ham
- 1/4 cup soy sauce
- 1 cup chopped cooked chicken breast

DIRECTIONS

1. Cook rice according to package directions. While rice is cooking, heat a wok or large skillet over medium-high heat. Pour in sesame oil and stir in onion. Fry until golden, then add garlic. When garlic is lightly browned, mix in shrimp, ham, and chicken. Fry until shrimp is pink.
2. Lower heat to medium and stir in celery, carrot, green pepper, and peas. Fry until vegetables are crisp-tender. Stir in beaten egg and cook just until egg is scrambled and firm.
3. When rice is done, mix thoroughly with vegetables and stir in soy sauce. Adjust seasoning to your preference and serve immediately.

BUFFALO CHICKEN FINGERS

Servings: 8 | Prep: 20m | Cooks: 20m | Total: 40m

NUTRITION FACTS

Calories: 125 | Carbohydrates: 10.7g | Fat: 2g | Protein: 15g | Cholesterol: 34mg

INGREDIENTS

- 4 skinless, boneless chicken breast halves - cut into finger-sized pieces
- 1/2 teaspoon salt
- 1/4 cup all-purpose flour
- 3/4 cup bread crumbs
- 1 teaspoon garlic powder
- 2 egg whites, beaten
- 1 teaspoon cayenne pepper
- 1 tablespoon water

DIRECTIONS

1. Preheat oven to 400 degrees F (205 degrees C). Coat a baking sheet with a nonstick spray.
2. In a bag, mix together flour, 1/2 teaspoon garlic powder, 1/2 teaspoon cayenne pepper, and 1/4 teaspoon salt. On a plate, mix the bread crumbs with the rest of the garlic powder, cayenne pepper, and salt.

3. Shake the chicken pieces with the seasoned flour. Beat egg whites with 1 tablespoon water, and place egg mixture in a shallow dish or bowl. Dip seasoned chicken in egg mixture, then roll in the seasoned bread crumb mixture. Place on prepared baking sheet.
4. Bake for about 8 minutes in the preheated oven. Use tongs to turn pieces over. Bake 8 minutes longer, or until chicken juices run clear.

MARRAKESH VEGETABLE CURRY
Servings: 6 | Prep: 15m | Cooks: 35m | Total: 50m

NUTRITION FACTS
Calories: 330 | Carbohydrates: 39g | Fat: 18g | Protein: 8g | Cholesterol: 0mg

INGREDIENTS
- 1 sweet potato, peeled and cubed
- 1 teaspoon ground cinnamon
- 1 medium eggplant, cubed
- 3/4 tablespoon sea salt
- 1 green bell pepper, chopped
- 3/4 teaspoon cayenne pepper
- 1 red bell pepper, chopped
- 1 (15 ounce) can garbanzo beans, drained
- 2 carrots, chopped
- 1/4 cup blanched almonds
- 1 onion, chopped
- 1 zucchini, sliced
- 6 tablespoons olive oil
- 2 tablespoons raisins
- 3 cloves garlic, minced
- 1 cup orange juice
- 1 teaspoon ground turmeric
- 10 ounces spinach
- 1 tablespoon curry powder

DIRECTIONS

1. In a large Dutch oven place sweet potato, eggplant, peppers, carrots, onion, and three tablespoons oil. Saute over medium heat for 5 minutes.
2. In a medium saucepan place 3 tablespoons olive oil, garlic, turmeric, curry powder, cinnamon, salt and pepper and saute over medium heat for 3 minutes.
3. Pour garlic and spice mixture into the Dutch oven with vegetables in it. Add the garbanzo beans, almonds, zucchini, raisins, and orange juice. Simmer 20 minutes, covered.
4. Add spinach to pot and cook for 5 more minutes. Serve!

PECAN PIE BARS
Servings: 36 | Prep: 20m | Cooks: 45m | Total: 1h5m

NUTRITION FACTS
Calories: 233 | Carbohydrates: 30.7g | Fat: 12g | Protein: 2.5g | Cholesterol: 21mg

INGREDIENTS

- 3 cups all-purpose flour
- 1 1/2 cups light corn syrup
- 1/2 cup white sugar
- 1 1/2 cups white sugar
- 1/2 teaspoon salt
- 3 tablespoons margarine, melted
- 1 cup margarine
- 1 1/2 teaspoons vanilla extract
- 4 eggs
- 2 1/2 cups chopped pecans

DIRECTIONS

1. Preheat oven to 350 degrees F (175 degrees C). Lightly grease a 10x15 inch jellyroll pan.
2. In a large bowl, stir together the flour, 1/2 cup sugar, and salt. Cut in 1 cup of margarine until mixture resembles coarse crumbs. Sprinkle the mixture evenly over the prepared pan, and press in firmly.
3. Bake for 20 minutes in the preheated oven.
4. While the crust is baking, prepare the filling. In a large bowl mix together the eggs, corn syrup, 1 1/2 cups sugar, 3 tablespoons margarine, and vanilla until smooth. Stir in the chopped pecans. Spread the filling evenly over the crust as soon as it comes out of the oven.
5. Bake for 25 minutes in the preheated oven, or until set. Allow to cool completely on a wire rack before slicing into bars.

GNOCCHI

Servings: 4 | Prep: 30m | Cooks: 30m | Total: 1h

NUTRITION FACTS

Calories: 329 | Carbohydrates: 67g | Fat: 2g | Protein: 9.7g | Cholesterol: 53mg

INGREDIENTS

- 2 potatoes
- 1 egg
- 2 cups all-purpose flour

DIRECTIONS

1. Bring a large pot of salted water to a boil. Peel potatoes and add to pot. Cook until tender but still firm, about 15 minutes. Drain, cool and mash with a fork or potato masher.
2. Combine 1 cup mashed potato, flour and egg in a large bowl. Knead until dough forms a ball. Shape small portions of the dough into long "snakes". On a floured surface, cut snakes into half-inch pieces.
3. Bring a large pot of lightly salted water to a boil. Drop in gnocchi and cook for 3 to 5 minutes or until gnocchi have risen to the top; drain and serve.

CHICKEN IN A POT

Servings: 4 | Prep: 20m | Cooks: 20m | Total: 40m

NUTRITION FACTS

INGREDIENTS

- 3/4 cup chicken broth
- 1 clove garlic, minced
- 1 1/2 tablespoons tomato paste
- 4 boneless, skinless chicken breast halves
- 1/4 teaspoon ground black pepper
- 3 tablespoons dry bread crumbs
- 1/2 teaspoon dried oregano
- 2 teaspoons olive oil
- 1/8 teaspoon salt
- 2 cups fresh sliced mushrooms

DIRECTIONS

1. In a medium bowl, combine the broth, tomato paste, ground black pepper, oregano, salt and garlic. Mix well and set aside.
2. Dredge the chicken in the bread crumbs, coating well. Heat the oil in a large skillet over medium high heat. Saute the chicken in the oil for 2 minutes per side, or until lightly browned.
3. Add the reserved broth mixture and the mushrooms to the skillet and bring to a boil. Then cover, reduce heat to low and simmer for 20 minutes. Remove chicken and set aside, covering to keep it warm.
4. Bring broth mixture to a boil and cook for 4 minutes, or until reduced to desired thickness. Spoon sauce over the chicken and serve.

WHOLE WHEAT AND HONEY PIZZA DOUGH

Servings: 12 | Prep: 10m | Cooks: 10m | Total: 20m

NUTRITION FACTS

Calories: 83 | Carbohydrates: 17.4g | Fat: 0.6g | Protein: 3.5g | Cholesterol: 0mg

INGREDIENTS

- 1 (.25 ounce) package active dry yeast
- 1/4 cup wheat germ
- 1 cup warm water
- 1 teaspoon salt
- 2 cups whole wheat flour
- 1 tablespoon honey

DIRECTIONS

1. Preheat oven to 350 degrees F (175 degrees C).
2. In a small bowl, dissolve yeast in warm water. Let stand until creamy, about 10 minutes.
3. In a large bowl combine flour, wheat germ and salt. Make a well in the middle and add honey and yeast mixture. Stir well to combine. Cover and set in a warm place to rise for a few minutes.
4. Roll dough on a floured pizza pan and poke a few holes in it with a fork.
5. Bake in preheated oven for 5 to 10 minutes, or until desired crispiness is achieved.

DIVINE HARD-BOILED EGGS

Servings: 12 | Prep: 5m | Cooks: 15m | Total: 2h50m

NUTRITION FACTS

Calories: 72 | Carbohydrates: 0.4g | Fat: 5g | Protein: 6.3g | Cholesterol: 186mg

INGREDIENTS

- 12 eggs

DIRECTIONS

1. Place eggs in a pot; pour enough water over the eggs to cover. Cover and turn stove to high; bring to a boil; turn off heat and place pot on a cool burner. Let the pot sit with the cover on for 15 minutes. Meanwhile, fill a large bowl halfway with cold water; transfer the eggs from the pot to the cold water. Replace the water with cold water as needed to keep cold until the eggs are completely cooled. Chill in refrigerator at least 2 hours before peeling.

SIMPLE COUNTRY RIBS

Servings: 4 | Prep: 10m | Cooks: 1h | Total: 1h10m

NUTRITION FACTS

Calories: 882 | Carbohydrates: 94.1g | Fat: 38.3g | Protein: 36.4g | Cholesterol: 150mg

INGREDIENTS

- 2 1/2 pounds pork spareribs
- 1 teaspoon salt
- 2 (18 ounce) bottles barbeque sauce
- 1/2 teaspoon ground black pepper
- 1 onion, quartered

DIRECTIONS

1. Place spareribs in a large stock pot with barbeque sauce, onion, salt, and pepper. Pour in enough water to cover. Bring to a low boil, and cook approximately 40 minutes.
2. Preheat grill for high heat.
3. Lightly oil grate. Remove spareribs from the stock pot, and place on the prepared grill. Use the barbeque sauce in the saucepan to baste ribs while cooking. Grill ribs, basting and turning frequently, for 20 minutes, or until nicely browned.

PEANUT NOODLES

Servings: 3 | Prep: 10m | Cooks: 15m | Total: 25m

NUTRITION FACTS

Calories: 568 | Carbohydrates: 70.1g | Fat: 24.8g | Protein: 19.7g | Cholesterol: 0mg

INGREDIENTS

- 8 ounces spaghetti
- 1/4 cup soy sauce
- 1 bunch green onions, sliced (white parts only)
- 1/4 cup hot water
- 2 tablespoons sesame oil
- 1 tablespoon cider vinegar
- 1 teaspoon minced fresh ginger root
- 1 teaspoon white sugar
- 1/3 cup peanut butter
- 1/4 teaspoon crushed red pepper flakes

DIRECTIONS

1. Cook pasta in a large pot of boiling water until done. Drain.
2. Meanwhile, combine oil and onions in a small skillet. Saute over low heat until tender. Add ginger; cook and stir for 1 to 2 minutes. Mix in peanut butter, soy sauce, water, vinegar, sugar, and red pepper flakes. Remove from heat.
3. Toss noodles with sauce, and serve.

GRILLED ASIAN CHICKEN

Servings: 12 | Prep: 15m | Cooks: 15m | Total: 50m | Additional: 20m

NUTRITION FACTS

Calories: 217 | Carbohydrates: 10.6g | Fat: 7.6g | Protein: 25.7g | Cholesterol: 67mg

INGREDIENTS

- 1/4 cup soy sauce
- 3 slices fresh ginger root
- 4 teaspoons sesame oil
- 2 cloves garlic, crushed
- 2 tablespoons honey
- 4 skinless, boneless chicken breast halves

DIRECTIONS

1. In a small microwave-safe bowl, combine the soy sauce, oil, honey, ginger root, and garlic. Heat in microwave on medium for 1 minute, then stir. Heat again for 30 seconds, watching closely to prevent boiling.
2. Place chicken breasts in a shallow dish. Pour soy sauce mixture over, and set aside to marinate for 15 minutes.
3. Preheat a grill for medium-high heat. Drain marinade from chicken into a small saucepan. Bring to a boil, and simmer over medium heat for 5 minutes. Set aside for basting.
4. Lightly oil the grill grate. Cook chicken on the prepared grill 6 to 8 minutes per side, or until juices run clear. Baste frequently with remaining marinade. Chicken will turn a beautiful golden brown.

BARBEQUED MARINATED FLANK STEAK

Servings: 6 | Prep: 15m | Cooks: 10m | Total: 8h25m

NUTRITION FACTS

Calories: 388 | Carbohydrates: 9.7g | Fat: 27.8g | Protein: 24.8g | Cholesterol: 47mg

INGREDIENTS

- 1/4 cup soy sauce
- 1/2 teaspoon garlic powder
- 3 tablespoons honey
- 1/2 cup vegetable oil
- 2 tablespoons distilled white vinegar
- 1 1/2 pounds flank steak
- 1/2 teaspoon ground ginger

DIRECTIONS

1. In a blender, combine the soy sauce, honey, vinegar, ginger, garlic powder, and vegetable oil.

2. Lay steak in a shallow glass or ceramic dish. Pierce both sides of the steak with a sharp fork. Pour marinade over steak, then turn and coat the other side. Cover, and refrigerate 8 hours, or overnight.
3. Preheat grill for high heat.
4. Place grate on highest level, and brush lightly with oil. Place steaks on the grill, and discard marinade. Grill steak for 10 minutes, turning once, or to desired doneness.

SNICKERDOODLES
Servings: 30 | Prep: 15m | Cooks: 10m | Total: 25m

NUTRITION FACTS
Calories: 150 | Carbohydrates: 19.8g | Fat: 7.3g | Protein: 1.6g | Cholesterol: 12mg

INGREDIENTS
- 1 cup shortening
- 2 teaspoons cream of tartar
- 1 1/2 cups white sugar
- 1/4 teaspoon salt
- 2 eggs
- 2 tablespoons white sugar
- 2 3/4 cups sifted all-purpose flour
- 2 teaspoons ground cinnamon
- 1 teaspoon baking soda

DIRECTIONS
1. Preheat oven to 400 degrees F (200 degrees C).
2. In a large bowl, mix together the shortening and 1 1/2 cups of white sugar until smooth. Stir in the eggs one at a time, blending well after each. Combine the flour, baking soda, cream of tartar and salt; stir into the batter until blended.
3. Roll the dough into balls the size of small walnuts. Roll in a mixture of 2 tablespoons sugar and 2 teaspoons cinnamon. Place 2 inches apart on an ungreased cookie sheet.
4. Bake in the preheated oven for 8 to 10 minutes or until lightly browned, but still soft.

YAKISOBA CHICKEN
Servings: 6 | Prep: 15m | Cooks: 15m | Total: 30m

NUTRITION FACTS
Calories: 295 | Carbohydrates: 40.7g | Fat: 4.8g | Protein: 26.3g | Cholesterol: 46mg

INGREDIENTS
- 1/2 teaspoon sesame oil
- 1/2 cup soy sauce
- 1 tablespoon canola oil
- 1 onion, sliced lengthwise into eighths
- 2 tablespoons chile paste
- 1/2 medium head cabbage, coarsely chopped
- 2 cloves garlic, chopped
- 2 carrots, coarsely chopped
- 4 skinless, boneless chicken breast halves - cut into 1 inch cubes
- 8 ounces soba noodles, cooked and drained

DIRECTIONS

1. In a large skillet combine sesame oil, canola oil and chili paste; stir-fry 30 seconds. Add garlic and stir fry an additional 30 seconds. Add chicken and 1/4 cup of the soy sauce and stir fry until chicken is no longer pink, about 5 minutes. Remove mixture from pan, set aside, and keep warm.
2.   In the emptied pan combine the onion, cabbage, and carrots. Stir-fry until cabbage begins to wilt, 2 to 3 minutes. Stir in the remaining soy sauce, cooked noodles, and the chicken mixture to pan and mix to blend. Serve and enjoy!

FAVORITE PEANUT BUTTER COOKIES
Servings: 54 | Prep: 30m | Cooks: 30m | Total: 1h

NUTRITION FACTS
Calories: 109 | Carbohydrates: 11g | Fat: 6.6g | Protein: 2.3g | Cholesterol: 7mg

INGREDIENTS

- 1 1/4 cups creamy peanut butter
- 1/2 teaspoon vanilla extract
- 1 cup margarine
- 2 1/4 cups all-purpose flour
- 3/4 cup white sugar
- 1 teaspoon baking powder
- 3/4 cup packed light brown sugar
- 1 teaspoon baking soda
- 2 eggs

DIRECTIONS

1. Preheat the oven to 375 degrees F (190 degrees C).
2. In a large bowl, cream together the peanut butter, margarine, brown sugar and white sugar. Beat in the eggs and vanilla. Combine the flour, baking powder and baking soda; stir into the peanut butter mixture. Form dough into walnut sized balls and place them 2 inches apart onto ungreased cookie sheets. Dip a fork into flour and criss cross each cookie to flatten slightly.
3. Bake for 12 to 15 minutes in the preheated oven, until just lightly browned. Allow cookies to cool on baking sheet for 5 minutes before removing to a wire rack to cool completely.

LONDON BROIL
Servings: 6 | Prep: 15m | Cooks: 15m | Total: 8h30m

NUTRITION FACTS
Calories: 222 | Carbohydrates: 3.8g | Fat: 9.1g | Protein: 30.1g | Cholesterol: 75mg

INGREDIENTS

- 3 cloves garlic, minced
- 1 teaspoon dried oregano
- 1/2 cup soy sauce
- 1 teaspoon ground black pepper
- 2 tablespoons vegetable oil
- 1 (2 pound) flank steak or round steak
- 2 tablespoons ketchup

DIRECTIONS

1. In a small bowl, mix together garlic, soy sauce, oil, ketchup, oregano, and black pepper. Pierce meat with a fork on both sides. Place meat and marinade in a large resealable plastic bag. Refrigerate 8 hours, or overnight.
2. Preheat grill for medium-high heat.
3. Lightly oil the grill grate. Place steak on the grill, and discard marinade. Cook for 5 to 8 minutes per side, depending on thickness. Do not overcook, as it is better on the rare side.

ASIAN BEEF SKEWERS
Servings: 6 | Prep: 30m | Cooks: 6m | Total: 2h40m

NUTRITION FACTS
Calories: 135 | Carbohydrates: 6.7g | Fat: 4.9g | Protein: 14.7g | Cholesterol: 25mg

INGREDIENTS
- 3 tablespoons hoisin sauce
- 2 cloves garlic, minced
- 3 tablespoons sherry
- 1 tablespoon minced fresh ginger root
- 1/4 cup soy sauce
- 1 1/2 pounds flank steak
- 1 teaspoon barbeque sauce
- skewers
- 2 green onions, chopped

DIRECTIONS

1. In a small bowl, mix together hoisin sauce, sherry, soy sauce, barbeque sauce, green onions, garlic, and ginger.
2. Cut flank steak across grain on a diagonal into 1/4 inch slices. Place slices in a 1 gallon resealable plastic bag. Pour hoisin sauce mixture over slices, and mix well. Refrigerate 2 hours, or overnight.
3. Preheat an outdoor grill for high heat. Discard marinade, and thread steak on skewers.
4. Oil the grill grate. Grill skewers 3 minutes per side, or to desired doneness.

FRIED RICE
Servings: 4 | Prep: 10m | Cooks: 30m | Total: 40m

NUTRITION FACTS
Calories: 516 | Carbohydrates: 63.5g | Fat: 20.7g | Protein: 17.3g | Cholesterol: 159mg

INGREDIENTS
- 1 1/3 cups uncooked white rice
- 3 teaspoons vegetable oil, divided
- 1 2/3 cups water
- 1/4 pound bacon, cut into strips
- 3 eggs, lightly beaten
- 1/8 cup soy sauce
- 1/4 teaspoon salt
- 1 (10 ounce) package frozen green peas, thawed

- 1/8 teaspoon ground black pepper
- 2 green onions, chopped

DIRECTIONS

1. In a saucepan bring water to a boil. Add rice and stir. Reduce heat, cover and simmer for 20 minutes. Meanwhile, season eggs with salt and pepper.
2. Heat 1 teaspoon oil in small frying pan, pour in eggs. Coat the bottom of the pan with the eggs, in order to cook them evenly; cook for about 3 minutes. Flip the eggs, cook one minute more and remove them to a cool surface. Let them cool, then cut them into thin slices. Set aside.
3. Place bacon in a large, deep skillet. Cook over medium high heat until evenly brown. Drain, crumble and set aside.
4. Spoon remaining 2 teaspoons oil into the skillet with the bacon fat. Stir in rice; break up any clumps and toss to coat with oil. Stir in bacon, soy sauce, peas, eggs and green onions. Stir and cook until heated through, approximately 3 minutes.

PICO DE GALLO

Servings: 4 | Prep: 20m | Cooks: 30m | Total: 50m

NUTRITION FACTS

Calories: 21 | Carbohydrates: 4.7g | Fat: 0.1g | Protein: 0.8g | Cholesterol: 0mg

INGREDIENTS

- 1 medium tomato, diced
- 1 green onion, finely chopped
- 1 onion, finely chopped
- 1/2 teaspoon garlic powder
- 1/2 fresh jalapeno pepper, seeded and chopped
- 1/8 teaspoon salt
- 2 sprigs fresh cilantro, finely chopped
- 1/8 teaspoon pepper

DIRECTIONS

1. In a medium bowl, combine tomato, onion, jalapeno pepper (to taste,) cilantro and green onion. Season with garlic powder, salt and pepper. Stir until evenly distributed. Refrigerate for 30 minutes.

PORCUPINES

Servings: 5 | Prep: 30m | Cooks: 1h | Total: 1h30m

NUTRITION FACTS

Calories: 275 | Carbohydrates: 21.1g | Fat: 12.8g | Protein: 18.5g | Cholesterol: 55mg

INGREDIENTS

- 1 pound lean ground beef
- 1/2 teaspoon celery salt
- 1/2 cup uncooked white rice
- 1/8 teaspoon garlic powder
- 1/2 cup water
- 1/8 teaspoon ground black pepper
- 1/2 cup chopped onion
- 1 (15 ounce) can tomato sauce

- 1 teaspoon salt
- 1 cup water

DIRECTIONS

1. In a large bowl, combine the ground beef, rice, 1/2 cup of water and onion. Blend in salt, celery salt, garlic powder and pepper. Mix well. Shape into 1 1/2 inch balls.
2. Preheat oven to 350 degrees F (175 degrees C). In a large skillet over medium heat, brown the meatballs; drain fat.
3. In an 11x7 inch baking dish, combine the tomato sauce and 1 cup of water. Place the browned meatballs into the tomato sauce, turning to coat well.
4. Cover and bake in a preheated oven for 45 minutes. Uncover, and cook for an additional 15 minutes.

EASIEST POT ROAST EVER

Servings: 6 | Prep: 10m | Cooks: 5h | Total: 5h10m

NUTRITION FACTS

Calories: 526 | Carbohydrates: 42.4g | Fat: 25.3g | Protein: 31.7g | Cholesterol: 103mg

INGREDIENTS

- 3 pounds beef roast
- 2 stalks celery
- 6 potatoes
- 3 cubes beef bouillon
- 1 1/2 cups baby carrots
- 1/2 cup water
- 1 yellow onion

DIRECTIONS

1. Cut up potatoes, onions, and celery in to fairly large chunks and place in a slow cooker. Put roast on top of vegetables. Place 3 bouillon cubes randomly on top of roast and pour in water.
2. Cover, and cook on low for 6 to 8 hours or High for 4 to 5 hours.

MUSHROOM SLOW COOKER ROAST BEEF

Servings: 8 | Prep: 5m | Cooks: 9h | Total:9h55m

NUTRITION FACTS

Calories: 388 | Carbohydrates: 6.2g | Fat: 28.1g | Protein: 24.4g | Cholesterol: 82mg

INGREDIENTS

- 1 pound sliced fresh mushrooms
- 1 (12 fluid ounce) bottle beer
- 1 (4 pound) standing beef rib roast
- ground black pepper
- 1 (1.25 ounce) envelope onion soup mix

DIRECTIONS

1. Place the mushrooms in the bottom of a slow cooker; set the roast atop the mushrooms; sprinkle the onion soup mix over the beef and pour the beer over everything; season with black pepper. Set slow cooker to LOW; cook 9 to 10 hours until the meat is easily pulled apart with a fork.

ANGEL FOOD CAKE

Servings: 14 | Prep: 30m | Cooks: 45m | Total: 1h15m

NUTRITION FACTS

Calories: 136 | Carbohydrates: 29.9g | Fat: 0.1g | Protein: 4g | Cholesterol: 0mg

INGREDIENTS

- 1 cup cake flour
- 1 1/2 cups white sugar
- 12 egg whites
- 1 1/2 teaspoons vanilla extract
- 1 1/2 teaspoons cream of tartar
- 1/2 teaspoon salt

DIRECTIONS

1. Preheat the oven to 375 degrees F (190 degrees C). Be sure that your 10 inch tube pan is clean and dry. Any amount of oil or residue could deflate the egg whites. Sift together the flour, and 3/4 cup of the sugar, set aside.
2. In a large bowl, whip the egg whites along with the vanilla, cream of tartar and salt, to medium stiff peaks. Gradually add the remaining sugar while continuing to whip to stiff peaks. When the egg white mixture has reached its maximum volume, fold in the sifted ingredients gradually, one third at a time. Do not overmix. Put the batter into the tube pan.
3. Bake for 40 to 45 minutes in the preheated oven, until the cake springs back when touched. Balance the tube pan upside down on the top of a bottle, to prevent decompression while cooling. When cool, run a knife around the edge of the pan and invert onto a plate.

BARBEQUED RIBS

Servings: 8 | Prep: 30m | Cooks: 3h | Total: 11h30m | Additional: 8h

NUTRITION FACTS

Calories: 588 | Carbohydrates: 18.9g | Fat: 37.5g | Protein: 44.2g | Cholesterol: 170mg

INGREDIENTS

- 4 pounds baby back pork ribs
- 1/2 cup cider vinegar
- 4 cloves garlic, sliced
- 1/2 cup ketchup
- 1 tablespoon white sugar
- 1/4 cup chili sauce
- 1 tablespoon paprika
- 1/4 cup Worcestershire sauce
- 2 teaspoons salt
- 1 tablespoon lemon juice
- 2 teaspoons ground black pepper
- 2 tablespoons onion, chopped
- 2 teaspoons chili powder
- 1/2 teaspoon dry mustard
- 2 teaspoons ground cumin

- 1 clove crushed garlic
- 1/2 cup dark brown sugar

DIRECTIONS

1. Preheat oven to 300 degrees F (150 degrees C). Place ribs on a rack in a shallow roasting pan. Scatter 4 cloves of sliced garlic over ribs. Cover, and bake for 2 1/2 hours. Cool slightly.
2. In a small bowl, mix together white sugar, paprika, salt, black pepper, chili powder, and ground cumin. Rub spices over cooled ribs. Cover, and refrigerate overnight.
3. In a small saucepan, mix together brown sugar, cider vinegar, ketchup, chili sauce, Worcestershire sauce, lemon juice, onion, dry mustard, and 1 clove garlic. Simmer over medium-low heat, uncovered, for 1 hour. Reserve a small amount for basting; the remainder is a dipping sauce.
4. Preheat grill for medium heat.
5. Place ribs on grill. Grill, covered, for about 12 minutes, basting with the reserved sauce, until nicely browned and glazed. Serve with remaining sauce for dipping.

QUICK GNOCCHI

Servings: 2 | Prep: 10m | Cooks: 5m | Total: 15m

NUTRITION FACTS

Calories: 462 | Carbohydrates: 91.3g | Fat: 3.5g | Protein: 14.8g | Cholesterol: 93mg

INGREDIENTS

- 1 cup dry potato flakes
- 1 teaspoon salt
- 1 cup boiling water
- 1/8 teaspoon ground black pepper
- 1 egg, beaten
- 1 1/2 cups all-purpose flour

DIRECTIONS

1. Place potato flakes in a medium-size bowl. Pour in boiling water; stir until blended. Let cool.
2. Stir in egg, salt, and pepper. Blend in enough flour to make a fairly stiff dough. Turn dough out on a well floured board. Knead lightly.
3. Divide dough in half. Shape each half into a long thin roll, the thickness of a breadstick. With a knife dipped in flour, cut into bite-size pieces.
4. Place a few gnocchi in boiling water. As the gnocchi rise to the top of the pot, remove them with a slotted spoon. Repeat until all are cooked.

MEDITERRANEAN LEMON CHICKEN

Servings: 6 | Prep: 15m | Cooks: 50m | Total: 1h5m

NUTRITION FACTS

Calories: 241 | Carbohydrates: 2.8g | Fat: 11.8g | Protein: 30.6g | Cholesterol: 105mg

INGREDIENTS

- 1 lemon
- 1/4 teaspoon salt
- 2 teaspoons dried oregano
- 1/4 teaspoon ground black pepper
- 3 cloves garlic, minced

- 6 chicken legs
- 1 tablespoon olive oil

DIRECTIONS

1. Preheat oven to 425 degrees F (220 degrees C).
2. In a 9x13 inch baking dish, grate the peel from 1/2 the lemon, squeeze out the juice (about 1/4 cup) and add to peel with the oregano, garlic, oil, salt and pepper. Stir until mixed.
3. Remove skin from chicken pieces and discard. Coat chicken pieces with the lemon mixture and arrange, bone-side up, in the baking dish. Cover dish and bake for 20 minutes. Turn and baste chicken.
4. Reduce heat to 400 degrees F (205 degrees C) and bake uncovered, basting every 10 minutes, for about 30 more minutes. Serve chicken with pan juices.

PERFECT SUSHI RICE

Servings: 15 | Prep: 5m | Cooks: 20m | Total: 45m

NUTRITION FACTS

Calories: 112 | Carbohydrates: 23.5g | Fat: 1g | Protein: 1.7g | Cholesterol: 0mg

INGREDIENTS

- 2 cups uncooked glutinous white rice (sushi rice)
- 1 tablespoon vegetable oil
- 3 cups water
- 1/4 cup white sugar
- 1/2 cup rice vinegar
- 1 teaspoon salt

DIRECTIONS

1. Rinse the rice in a strainer or colander until the water runs clear. Combine with water in a medium saucepan. Bring to a boil, then reduce the heat to low, cover and cook for 20 minutes. Rice should be tender and water should be absorbed. Cool until cool enough to handle.
2. In a small saucepan, combine the rice vinegar, oil, sugar and salt. Cook over medium heat until the sugar dissolves. Cool, then stir into the cooked rice. When you pour this in to the rice it will seem very wet. Keep stirring and the rice will dry as it cools.

ROSEMARY BRAISED LAMB SHANKS

Servings: 6 | Prep: 30m | Cooks: 2h | Total: 2h30m

NUTRITION FACTS

Calories: 481 | Carbohydrates: 17.6g | Fat: 21.8g | Protein: 30.3g | Cholesterol: 93mg

INGREDIENTS

- 6 lamb shanks
- 1 (750 milliliter) bottle red wine
- salt and pepper to taste
- 1 (28 ounce) can whole peeled tomatoes with juice
- 2 tablespoons olive oil
- 1 (10.5 ounce) can condensed chicken broth
- 2 onions, chopped
- 1 (10.5 ounce) can beef broth

- 3 large carrots, cut into 1/4 inch rounds
- 5 teaspoons chopped fresh rosemary
- 10 cloves garlic, minced
- 2 teaspoons chopped fresh thyme

DIRECTIONS

1. Sprinkle shanks with salt and pepper. Heat oil in heavy large pot or Dutch oven over medium-high heat. Working in batches, cook shanks until brown on all sides, about 8 minutes. Transfer shanks to plate.
2. Add onions, carrots and garlic to pot and saute until golden brown, about 10 minutes. Stir in wine, tomatoes, chicken broth and beef broth. Season with rosemary and thyme. Return shanks to pot, pressing down to submerge. Bring to a boil, then reduce heat to medium-low. Cover, and simmer until meat is tender, about 2 hours.
3. Remove cover from pot. Simmer about 20 minutes longer. Transfer shanks to platter, place in a warm oven. Boil juices in pot until thickened, about 15 minutes. Spoon over shanks.

ONION RICE

Servings: 6 | Prep: 10m | Cooks: 30m | Total: 40m

NUTRITION FACTS

Calories: 141 | Carbohydrates: 26.6g | Fat: 2.5g | Protein: 2.4g | Cholesterol: 0mg

INGREDIENTS

- 1 tablespoon vegetable oil
- 1 teaspoon ground black pepper
- 1 red onion, chopped
- 2 cups chicken broth
- 1 cup long-grain white rice

DIRECTIONS

1. Heat the oil in a saucepan over medium heat. Stir in the onion, and cook until almost tender. Stir in rice, and continue cooking until coated with oil. When onion is tender and rice begins to brown lightly, season with pepper, and pour in the broth. Bring to a boil. Reduce heat to low, cover, and simmer 20 minutes.

APRICOT CHICKEN

Servings: 6 | Prep: 30m | Cooks: 1h | Total: 1h30m

NUTRITION FACTS

Calories: 456 | Carbohydrates: 55.7g | Fat: 13.8g | Protein: 28.5g | Cholesterol: 68mg

INGREDIENTS

- 6 skinless, boneless chicken breast halves
- 1 (10 fluid ounce) bottle Russian-style salad dressing
- 1 ½ (1 ounce) packages dry onion soup mix
- 1 cup apricot preserves

DIRECTIONS

1. Preheat oven to 350 degrees F (175 degrees C).
2. Place the chicken pieces in a 4 quart casserole dish. Mix the soup mix, dressing and jam together, and pour over the chicken.

3. Cover dish and bake for 1 hour in preheated oven.

GRILLED ROCK LOBSTER TAILS
Servings: 2 | Prep: 15m | Cooks: 12m | Total: 27m

NUTRITION FACTS

Calories: 742 | Carbohydrates: 4.3g | Fat: 60.9g | Protein: 44.3g | Cholesterol: 169mg

INGREDIENTS

- 1 tablespoon lemon juice
- 1/8 teaspoon white pepper
- 1/2 cup olive oil
- 1/8 teaspoon garlic powder
- 1 teaspoon salt
- 2 (10 ounce) rock lobster tails
- 1 teaspoon paprika

DIRECTIONS

1. Preheat grill for high heat.
2. Squeeze lemon juice into a small bowl, and slowly whisk in olive oil. Whisk in salt, paprika, white pepper, and garlic powder. Split lobster tails lengthwise with a large knife, and brush flesh side of tail with marinade.
3. Lightly oil grill grate. Place tails, flesh side down, on preheated grill. Cook for 10 to 12 minutes, turning once, and basting frequently with marinade. Discard any remaining marinade. Lobster is done when opaque and firm to the touch.

GRILLED PORTOBELLO MUSHROOMS
Servings: 3 | Prep: 10m | Cooks: 10m | Total: 1h20m

NUTRITION FACTS

Calories: 217 | Carbohydrates: 11g | Fat: 19g | Protein: 3.2g | Cholesterol: 0mg

INGREDIENTS

- 3 portobello mushrooms
- 4 cloves garlic, minced
- 1/4 cup canola oil
- 4 tablespoons balsamic vinegar
- 3 tablespoons chopped onion

DIRECTIONS

1. Clean mushrooms and remove stems, reserve for other use. Place caps on a plate with the gills up.
2. In a small bowl, combine the oil, onion, garlic and vinegar. Pour mixture evenly over the mushroom caps and let stand for 1 hour.
3. Grill over hot grill for 10 minutes. Serve immediately.

ORANGE CHICKEN STIR FRY
Servings: 4 | Prep: 10m | Cooks: 35m | Total: 45m

NUTRITION FACTS

Calories: 524 | Carbohydrates: 41.1g | Fat: 25.1g | Protein: 34.7g | Cholesterol: 68mg

INGREDIENTS

- 1 cup orange juice
- 3 tablespoons vegetable oil
- 1 tablespoon grated orange zest
- 4 skinless, boneless chicken breast halves - cut into 1 inch cubes
- 1/4 cup soy sauce
- 2 tablespoons all-purpose flour
- 1 teaspoon salt
- 1 cup bean sprouts (optional)
- 3 cloves garlic, chopped
- 1 (6 ounce) package crispy chow mein noodles
- 1 tablespoon brown sugar

DIRECTIONS

1. In a small bowl combine the orange juice, orange zest, soy sauce, salt, garlic and brown sugar. Mix well.
2. Heat oil in a large skillet or wok over medium high heat. When oil begins to bubble, add chicken. Saute until cooked through (no longer pink inside), about 7 to 10 minutes.
3. Add orange sauce mixture to chicken and cook until sauce begins to bubble. Add flour, a little bit at a time, until sauce has thickened to your liking. Add bean sprouts and cook for 1 minute; serve hot over chow mein noodles.

EASY GRILLED CHICKEN TERIYAKI
Servings: 4 | Prep: 15m | Cooks: 15m | Total: 1d | Additional: 1d

NUTRITION FACTS
Calories: 240 | Carbohydrates: 16.6g | Fat: 7.5g | Protein: 25.2g | Cholesterol: 67mg

INGREDIENTS

- 4 skinless, boneless chicken breast halves
- 2 teaspoons minced fresh garlic
- 1 cup teriyaki sauce
- 2 teaspoons sesame oil
- 1/4 cup lemon juice

DIRECTIONS

1. Place chicken, teriyaki sauce, lemon juice, garlic, and sesame oil in a large resealable plastic bag. Seal bag, and shake to coat. Place in refrigerator for 24 hours, turning every so often.
2. Preheat grill for high heat.
3. Lightly oil the grill grate. Remove chicken from bag, discarding any remaining marinade. Grill for 6 to 8 minutes each side, or until juices run clear when chicken is pierced with a fork.

MICROWAVE CARAMEL POPCORN
Servings: 16 | Prep: 5m | Cooks: 10m | Total: 15m

NUTRITION FACTS
Calories: 173 | Carbohydrates: 23.8g | Fat: 8.7g | Protein: 1.1g | Cholesterol: 0mg

INGREDIENTS

- 4 quarts popped popcorn

- 1/2 teaspoon salt
- 1 cup brown sugar
- 1 teaspoon vanilla extract
- 1/2 cup margarine
- 1/2 teaspoon baking soda
- 1/4 cup light corn syrup

DIRECTIONS

1. Place the popped popcorn into a large brown paper bag. Set aside.
2. In a 2 quart casserole dish, or other heat-proof glass dish, combine the brown sugar, margarine, corn syrup, salt and vanilla. Heat for 3 minutes in the microwave, then take out and stir until well blended. Return to the microwave, and cook for 1 1/2 minutes. Remove from microwave, and stir in the baking soda.
3. Pour syrup over the popcorn in the bag. Roll down the top once or twice to close the bag, and shake to coat the corn. Place bag into the microwave, and cook for 1 minute and 10 seconds. Remove, shake, flip the bag over, and return it to the microwave. Cook for another 1 minute and 10 seconds. Dump the popcorn out onto waxed paper, and let cool until coating is set. Store in an airtight container.

VEGGIE POT PIE

Servings: 6 | Prep: 30m | Cooks: 1h | Total: 1h30m

NUTRITION FACTS

Calories: 469 | Carbohydrates: 54.4g | Fat: 25g | Protein: 8.4g | Cholesterol: 0mg

INGREDIENTS

- 2 tablespoons olive oil
- 1 cup fresh green beans, trimmed and snapped into 1/2 inch pieces
- 1 onion, chopped
- 3 cups vegetable broth
- 8 ounces mushrooms
- 1 teaspoon kosher salt
- 1 clove garlic, minced
- 1 teaspoon ground black pepper
- 2 large carrots, diced
- 2 tablespoons cornstarch
- 2 potatoes, peeled and diced
- 2 tablespoons soy sauce
- 2 stalks celery, sliced 1/4 inch wide
- 1 recipe pastry for double-crust pie
- 2 cups cauliflower florets

DIRECTIONS

1. Preheat oven to 425 degrees F (220 degrees C).
2. Heat oil in a large skillet or saucepan. Cook onions, mushrooms, and garlic in oil for 3 to 5 minutes, stirring frequently. Stir in carrots, potatoes, and celery. Stir in cauliflower, green beans, and vegetable broth. Bring to a boil, then turn heat down to a simmer. Cook until vegetables are barely tender, about 5 minutes. Season with salt and pepper.

3. In a small bowl, mix the cornstarch, soy sauce, and 1/4 cup water until cornstarch is completely dissolved. Stir into vegetables, and cook until sauce thickens, about 3 minutes.
4. Roll out 1/2 of the dough to line an 11x7 inch baking dish. Pour the filling into the pastry lined dish. Roll out remaining dough, arrange over the filling, and seal and flute the edges.
5. Bake in preheated oven for 30 minutes, or until the crust is brown.

THREE BERRY PIE

Servings: 8 | Prep: 45m | Cooks: 45m | Total: 3h | Additional: 1h30m

NUTRITION FACTS

Calories: 361 | Carbohydrates: 48g | Fat: 17.7g | Protein: 3.8g | Cholesterol: 0mg

INGREDIENTS

- 2 cups all-purpose flour
- 2 cups fresh raspberries
- 1/2 teaspoon salt
- 1 1/2 cups fresh blueberries
- 2/3 cup shortening, chilled
- 1/2 cup white sugar
- 6 tablespoons cold water
- 3 tablespoons cornstarch
- 1 cup fresh strawberries, halved

DIRECTIONS

1. Combine the flour and salt. Using a pastry blender, cut in the shortening until the pieces are the size of small peas. Sprinkle 1 tablespoon of the water over part of the mixture, then gently toss with a fork. Push moistened portion to the side of the bowl. Repeat, using 1 tablespoon of water at a time, until all is moistened. Divide the dough in half. Form each half into a ball and flatten slightly. Wrap in plastic and refrigerate for at least 30 minutes.
2. Transfer one piece of dough to a lightly floured surface. Roll the dough from the center to the edges to form a 12-inch circle. Wrap the crust around the rolling pin. Unroll it onto a 9-inch pie plate. Ease the crust into the pie plate, being careful not to stretch it. Trim the bottom crust evenly with the rim of the pie plate, and return the pastry-lined pie plate to the refrigerator.
3. In a large mixing bowl, stir together the sugar and cornstarch. Add the strawberries, raspberries, and blueberries; gently toss until berries are coated. Allow fruit mixture to stand for about 15 minutes.
4. Preheat the oven to 375 degrees F (190 degrees C). Place a baking sheet in the oven to preheat.
5. Roll out the remaining pastry for the top crust. Stir the berry mixture and pour the filling into the pastry-lined pie plate. Place the top crust over the pie and trim the edges, leaving a 1/2-inch overhang. Fold the top crust under the bottom crust, pressing lightly to seal. Crimp the edges of the crust and cut vents in the top to allow steam to escape. To prevent over-browning, cover the edge of the pie with foil.
6. Bake in the preheated oven on the baking tray for 25 minutes. Remove the foil.
7. Bake for an additional 20 to 30 minutes, or until the filling is bubbling and the crust is golden. Cool on a wire rack.

GRECIAN PORK TENDERLOIN

Servings: 6 | Prep: 15m | Cooks: 30m | Total: 2h45m | Additional: 2h

NUTRITION FACTS

Calories: 404 | Carbohydrates: 9.1g | Fat: 31.1g | Protein: 24.3g | Cholesterol: 65mg

INGREDIENTS

- 1 1/2 cups fresh lime juice
- 2 teaspoons salt
- 3/4 cup olive oil
- 6 tablespoons dried oregano
- 6 cloves garlic, sliced
- 2 (1 pound) pork tenderloins

DIRECTIONS

1. Place lime juice, olive oil, garlic, salt, and oregano in a large resealable plastic bag. Shake sealed bag until ingredients are well mixed. Taste the marinade for tartness. If too tart, add a little more oil. Not enough zing, add more lime. The garlic and salt flavors should also be up front, yet not overpowering. Place tenderloins in the bag, seal, and turn to coat. Marinate in the refrigerator for 2 to 5 hours.
2. Preheat grill for medium heat.
3. Lightly oil the grill grate, and discard marinade. Grill tenderloins for 20 to 30 minutes, turning once, or to desired doneness.

GRANDMA'S GINGERSNAPS

Servings: 36 | Prep: 15m | Cooks: 10m | Total: 30m | Additional: 5m

NUTRITION FACTS

Calories: 100 | Carbohydrates: 15.5g | Fat: 4g | Protein: 1g | Cholesterol: 5mg

INGREDIENTS

- 3/4 cup margarine
- 1 tablespoon ground ginger
- 1 cup white sugar
- 1 teaspoon ground cinnamon
- 1 egg
- 2 teaspoons baking soda
- 1/4 cup molasses
- 1/2 teaspoon salt
- 2 cups all-purpose flour
- 1/2 cup white sugar for decoration

DIRECTIONS

1. Preheat oven to 350 degrees F (175 degrees C).
2. In a medium bowl, cream together the margarine and 1 cup white sugar until smooth. Beat in the egg and molasses until well blended. Combine the flour, ginger, cinnamon, baking soda and salt; stir into the molasses mixture to form a dough. Roll dough into 1 inch balls and roll the balls in the remaining sugar. Place cookies 2 inches apart onto ungreased cookie sheets.
3. Bake for 8 to 10 minutes in the preheated oven. Allow cookies to cool on baking sheet for 5 minutes before removing to a wire rack to cool completely.

SLOW COOKER HONEY GARLIC CHICKEN

Servings: 10 | Prep: 20m | Cooks: 4h | Total: 4h20m

NUTRITION FACTS

Calories: 235 | Carbohydrates: 34.4g | Fat: 6g | Protein: 13g | Cholesterol: 42mg

INGREDIENTS

- 1 tablespoon vegetable oil
- 2 cloves garlic, crushed
- 10 boneless, skinless chicken thighs
- 1 tablespoon minced fresh ginger root
- 3/4 cup honey
- 1 (20 ounce) can pineapple tidbits, drained with juice reserved
- 3/4 cup lite soy sauce
- 2 tablespoons cornstarch
- 3 tablespoons ketchup
- 1/4 cup water

DIRECTIONS

1. Heat oil in a skillet over medium heat, and cook chicken thighs just until evenly browned on all sides. Place thighs in a slow cooker.
2. In a bowl, mix honey, soy sauce, ketchup, garlic, ginger, and reserved pineapple juice. Pour into the slow cooker.
3. Cover, and cook 4 hours on High. Stir in pineapple tidbits just before serving.
4. Mix the cornstarch and water in a small bowl. Remove thighs from slow cooker. Blend the cornstarch mixture into remaining sauce in the slow cooker to thicken. Serve sauce over the chicken.

CHICKEN LO MEIN

Servings: 4 | Prep: 45m | Cooks: 30m | Total: 2h15m | Additional: 1h

NUTRITION FACTS

Calories: 599 | Carbohydrates: 78.6g | Fat: 14.7g | Protein: 38g | Cholesterol: 61mg

INGREDIENTS

- 4 skinless, boneless chicken breast halves - cut into thin strips
- 2 tablespoons cornstarch
- 5 teaspoons white sugar, divided
- 1 (12 ounce) package uncooked linguine pasta
- 3 tablespoons rice wine vinegar
- 2 tablespoons vegetable oil, divided
- 1/2 cup soy sauce, divided
- 2 tablespoons minced fresh ginger root
- 1 1/4 cups chicken broth
- 1 tablespoon minced garlic
- 1 cup water
- 1/2 pound fresh shiitake mushrooms, stemmed and sliced
- 1 tablespoon sesame oil
- 6 green onions, sliced diagonally into 1/2 inch pieces
- 1/2 teaspoon ground black pepper

DIRECTIONS

1. In a medium, non-reactive bowl, combine the chicken with 2 1/2 teaspoons of white sugar, 1 1/2 tablespoons vinegar and 1/4 cup soy sauce. Mix this together and coat the chicken well. Cover and let marinate in the refrigerator for at least 1 hour.
2. In another medium bowl, combine the chicken broth, water, sesame oil and ground black pepper with the remaining sugar, vinegar and soy sauce. In a separate small bowl, dissolve the cornstarch with some of this mixture and slowly add to the bulk of the mixture, stirring well. Set aside.
3. Cook the linguine according to package directions, drain and set aside. Heat 1 tablespoon of the vegetable oil in a wok or large saucepan over high heat until it starts to smoke. Add the chicken and stir-fry for 4 to 5 minutes, or until browned. Transfer this and all juices to a warm plate.
4. Heat the remaining vegetable oil in the wok or pan over high heat. Add the ginger, garlic, mushrooms and green onions, and stir-fry for 30 seconds. Add the reserved sauce mixture and then the chicken. Simmer until the sauce begins to thicken, about 2 minutes. Add the reserved noodles and toss gently, coating everything well with the sauce.

QUICK AND EASY PANCIT
Servings: 6 | Prep: 20m | Cooks: 20m | Total: 40m
NUTRITION FACTS
Calories: 369 | Carbohydrates: 65.1g | Fat: 4.9g | Protein: 18.1g | Cholesterol: 35mg
INGREDIENTS
- 1 (12 ounce) package dried rice noodles
- 1 small head cabbage, thinly sliced
- 1 teaspoon vegetable oil
- 4 carrot, thinly sliced
- 1 onion, finely diced
- 1/4 cup soy sauce
- 3 cloves garlic, minced
- 2 lemons - cut into wedges, for garnish
- 2 cups diced cooked chicken breast meat

DIRECTIONS
1. Place the rice noodles in a large bowl, and cover with warm water. When soft, drain, and set aside.
2. Heat oil in a wok or large skillet over medium heat. Saute onion and garlic until soft. Stir in chicken cabbage, carrots and soy sauce. Cook until cabbage begins to soften. Toss in noodles, and cook until heated through, stirring constantly. Transfer pancit to a serving dish and garnish with quartered lemons.

BARBEQUE PORK TWO WAYS
Servings: 8 | Prep: 15m | Cooks: 8h | Total: 8h15m
NUTRITION FACTS
Calories: 279 | Carbohydrates: 24.7g | Fat: 13.6g | Protein: 15.8g | Cholesterol: 56mg
INGREDIENTS
- 2 1/2 pounds pork shoulder
- 1/2 teaspoon salt
- 1/2 cup chopped onion
- 1/4 teaspoon ground black pepper

- 1 clove garlic, minced
- 2 cups ketchup
- 1/4 cup brown sugar
- 1/4 cup Worcestershire sauce
- 1 teaspoon dry mustard

DIRECTIONS

1. Cut boneless pork shoulder crosswise into 1/4 inch slices. Partially freezing it will make slicing easier.
2. In the slow cooker, combine sliced pork, onion, garlic, brown sugar, dry mustard, salt, pepper, ketchup, and Worcestershire sauce; mix well, and cover. Cook on Low, stirring occasionally, for 6 to 8 hours or until the meat is tender.
3. OR : In a Dutch oven or large saucepan, combine pork, onion, garlic, brown sugar, dry mustard, salt, pepper, ketchup, and Worcestershire sauce; mix well. Bring to a boil, reduce heat, and cover. Simmer, stirring occasionally, for 2 1/2 to 3 hours or until pork is tender.

LENTILS AND SPINACH

Servings: 4 | Prep: 10m | Cooks: 55m | Total: 1h5m

NUTRITION FACTS

Calories: 165 | Carbohydrates: 24g | Fat: 4.3g | Protein: 9.7g | Cholesterol: 0mg

INGREDIENTS

- 1 tablespoon vegetable oil
- 1 (10 ounce) package frozen spinach
- 2 white onions, halved and sliced into 1/2 rings
- 1 teaspoon salt
- 3 cloves garlic, minced
- 1 teaspoon ground cumin
- 1/2 cup lentils
- freshly ground black pepper to taste
- 2 cups water
- 2 cloves garlic, crushed

DIRECTIONS

1. Heat oil in a heavy pan over medium heat. Saute onion for 10 minutes or so, until it begins to turn golden. Add minced garlic and saute for another minute or so.
2. Add lentils and water to the saucepan. Bring mixture to a boil. Cover, lower heat, and simmer about 35 minutes, until lentils are soft (this may take less time, depending on your water and the lentils).
3. Meanwhile cook the spinach in microwave according to package directions. Add spinach, salt and cumin to the saucepan. Cover and simmer until all is heated, about ten minutes. Grind in plenty of pepper and press in extra garlic to taste.

EGG IN A HOLE

Servings: 1 | Prep: 1m | Cooks: 4m | Total: 5m

NUTRITION FACTS

Calories: 231 | Carbohydrates: 13.1g | Fat: 15.9g | Protein: 8.7g | Cholesterol: 208mg

INGREDIENTS

- 1 1/2 teaspoons bacon grease
- 1 egg
- 1 slice bread
- salt and ground black pepper to taste

DIRECTIONS

1. Melt the bacon grease in a non-stick pan over low heat.
2. Cut a 1 1/2 to 2-inch hole from the center of the bread slice; lay in the hot skillet. When the side facing down is lightly toasted, about 2 minutes, flip and crack the egg into the hole; season with salt and pepper. Continue to cook until the egg is cooked and mostly firm. Flip again and cook 1 minute more to assure doneness on both sides. Serve immediately.

ESPINACAS CON GARBANZOS (SPINACH WITH GARBANZO BEANS)

Servings: 4 | Prep: 15m | Cooks: 10m | Total: 25m

NUTRITION FACTS

Calories: 169 | Carbohydrates: 26g | Fat: 4.9g | Protein: 7.3g | Cholesterol: 0mg

INGREDIENTS

- 1 tablespoon extra-virgin olive oil
- 1 (12 ounce) can garbanzo beans, drained
- 4 cloves garlic, minced
- 1/2 teaspoon cumin
- 1/2 onion, diced
- 1/2 teaspoon salt
- 1 (10 ounce) box frozen chopped spinach, thawed and drained well

DIRECTIONS

1. Heat the olive oil in a skillet over medium-low heat. Cook the garlic and onion in the oil until translucent, about 5 minutes. Stir in the spinach, garbanzo beans, cumin, and salt. Use your stirring spoon to lightly mash the beans as the mixture cooks. Allow to cook until thoroughly heated.

RONALDO'S BEEF CARNITAS

Servings: 12 | Prep: 10m | Cooks: 4h | Total: 4h10m

NUTRITION FACTS

Calories: 218 | Carbohydrates: 1.4g | Fat: 13.8g | Protein: 20.8g | Cholesterol: 70mg

INGREDIENTS

- 4 pounds chuck roast
- 1/2 teaspoon ground cumin
- 1 (4 ounce) can green chile peppers, chopped
- 2 cloves garlic, minced
- 2 tablespoons chili powder
- salt to taste
- 1/2 teaspoon dried oregano

DIRECTIONS

1. Preheat oven to 300 degrees F (150 degrees C).
2. Place roast on heavy foil large enough to enclose the meat. In a small bowl, combine the green chile peppers, chili powder, oregano, cumin, garlic and salt to taste. Mix well and rub over the meat.
3. Totally wrap the meat in the foil and place in a roasting pan.
4. Bake at 300 degrees F (150 degrees C) for 3 1/2 to 4 hours, or until the roast just falls apart with a fork. Remove from oven and shred using two forks.

VEGAN BEAN TACO FILLING
Servings: 8 | Prep: 15m | Cooks: 15m | Total: 30m

NUTRITION FACTS
Calories: 142 | Carbohydrates: 24g | Fat: 2.5g | Protein: 7.5g | Cholesterol: 0mg

INGREDIENTS
- 1 tablespoon olive oil
- 1 1/2 tablespoons cumin
- 1 onion, diced
- 1 teaspoon paprika
- 2 cloves garlic, minced
- 1 teaspoon cayenne pepper
- 1 bell pepper, chopped
- 1 teaspoon chili powder
- 2 (14.5 ounce) cans black beans, rinsed, drained, and mashed
- 1 cup salsa
- 2 tablespoons yellow cornmeal

DIRECTIONS
1. Heat olive oil in a medium skillet over medium heat. Stir in onion, garlic, and bell pepper; cook until tender. Stir in mashed beans. Add the cornmeal. Mix in cumin, paprika, cayenne, chili powder, and salsa. Cover, and cook 5 minutes.

SUKHOTHAI PAD THAI
Servings: 8 | Prep: 20m | Cooks: 10m | Total: 30m

NUTRITION FACTS
Calories: 619 | Carbohydrates: 64.1g | Fat: 34g | Protein: 19.5g | Cholesterol: 93mg

INGREDIENTS
- 1/2 cup white sugar
- 1 1/2 tablespoons white sugar
- 1/2 cup distilled white vinegar
- 1 1/2 teaspoons salt
- 1/4 cup soy sauce
- 1 1/2 cups ground peanuts
- 2 tablespoons tamarind pulp
- 1 1/2 teaspoons ground, dried oriental radish
- 1 (12 ounce) package dried rice noodles
- 1/2 cup chopped fresh chives
- 1/2 cup vegetable oil

- 1 tablespoon paprika
- 1 1/2 teaspoons minced garlic
- 2 cups fresh bean sprouts
- 4 eggs
- 1 lime, cut into wedges
- 1 (12 ounce) package firm tofu, cut into 1/2 inch strips

DIRECTIONS

1. To prepare Pad Thai sauce: In a medium saucepan over medium heat, blend sugar, vinegar, soy sauce and tamarind pulp.
2. To make Pad Thai: Soak rice noodles in cold water until soft; drain. In a large skillet or wok over medium heat, warm oil and add garlic and eggs; scramble the eggs. Add tofu and stir until well mixed; add noodles and stir until cooked.
3. Stir in Pad Thai sauce, 1 1/2 tablespoons sugar and 1 1/2 teaspoons salt. Stir in peanuts and ground radish. Remove from heat and add chives and paprika.
4. Serve with lime and bean sprouts on the side.

SWEET AND SOUR MEATBALLS
Servings: 5 | Prep: 5m | Cooks: 15m | Total: 20m

NUTRITION FACTS
Calories: 601 | Carbohydrates: 70.5g | Fat: 26.3g | Protein: 20.4g | Cholesterol: 114mg

INGREDIENTS

- 1 pound ground beef
- 1/2 cup cider vinegar
- 1 egg
- 1/2 cup ketchup
- 1 onion, chopped
- 2 tablespoons cornstarch
- 1 cup dry bread crumbs
- 1 cup brown sugar
- salt and pepper to taste
- 2 tablespoons soy sauce
- 1 cup water

DIRECTIONS

1. In a large bowl, combine beef, egg, onion, bread crumbs, salt and pepper. Roll into meatballs about 1 to 1 1/2 inches in size.
2. In a large skillet over medium heat, saute the meatballs until browned on all sides.
3. In a separate medium bowl, mix together the water, vinegar, ketchup, cornstarch, sugar and soy sauce. Pour over the meatballs, and allow sauce to thicken. Continue to heat until the sauce just starts to bubble.

PUTTANESCA
Servings: 4 | Prep: 25m | Cooks: 15m | Total: 40m

NUTRITION FACTS
Calories: 490 | Carbohydrates: 38.7g | Fat: 34g | Protein: 9.3g | Cholesterol: 44mg

INGREDIENTS

- 8 ounces pasta
- 2 tablespoons tomato paste
- 1/2 cup olive oil
- 3 tablespoons capers
- 3 cloves garlic, minced
- 20 Greek olives, pitted and coarsely chopped
- 2 cups chopped tomatoes, pushed through a sieve
- 1/2 teaspoon crushed red pepper flakes
- 4 anchovy filets, rinsed and chopped

DIRECTIONS

1. Bring a large pot of lightly salted water to a boil. Cook pasta in boiling water for 8 to 10 minutes or until al dente; drain.
2. Heat oil in a skillet over low heat; cook garlic in oil until golden. Add sieved tomatoes, and cook 5 minutes. Stir in anchovies, tomato paste, capers, olives, and red pepper flakes. Cook 10 minutes, stirring occasionally.
3. Toss pasta with sauce, and serve.

CHINESE CHICKEN FRIED RICE
Servings: 7 | Prep: 25m | Cooks: 15m | Total: 40m

NUTRITION FACTS
Calories: 425 | Carbohydrates: 47.5g | Fat: 9.5g | Protein: 34.7g | Cholesterol: 134mg

INGREDIENTS

- 1/2 tablespoon sesame oil
- 1 large red bell pepper, diced
- 1 onion
- 3/4 cup fresh pea pods, halved
- 1 1/2 pounds cooked, cubed chicken meat
- 1/2 large green bell pepper, diced
- 2 tablespoons soy sauce
- 6 cups cooked white rice
- 2 large carrots, diced
- 2 eggs
- 2 stalks celery, chopped
- 1/3 cup soy sauce

DIRECTIONS

1. Heat oil in a large skillet over medium heat. Add onion and saute until soft, then add chicken and 2 tablespoons soy sauce and stir-fry for 5 to 6 minutes.
2. Stir in carrots, celery, red bell pepper, pea pods and green bell pepper and stir-fry another 5 minutes. Then add rice and stir thoroughly.
3. Finally, stir in scrambled eggs and 1/3 cup soy sauce, heat through and serve hot.

GINGERBREAD BISCOTTI
Servings: 48 | Prep: 25m | Cooks: 40m | Total: 1h5m

NUTRITION FACTS

Calories: 70 | Carbohydrates: 12.1g | Fat: 2g | Protein: 1.4g | Cholesterol: 12mg

INGREDIENTS

- 1/3 cup vegetable oil
- 1 tablespoon baking powder
- 1 cup white sugar
- 1 1/2 tablespoons ground ginger
- 3 eggs
- 3/4 tablespoon ground cinnamon
- 1/4 cup molasses
- 1/2 tablespoon ground cloves
- 2 1/4 cups all-purpose flour
- 1/4 teaspoon ground nutmeg
- 1 cup whole wheat flour

DIRECTIONS

1. Preheat the oven to 375 degrees F (190 degrees C). Grease a cookie sheet.
2. In a large bowl, mix together oil, sugar, eggs, and molasses. In another bowl, combine flours, baking powder, ginger, cinnamon, cloves, and nutmeg; mix into egg mixture to form a stiff dough.
3. Divide dough in half, and shape each half into a roll the length of the cookie. Place rolls on cookie sheet, and pat down to flatten the dough to 1/2 inch thickness.
4. Bake in preheated oven for 25 minutes. Remove from oven, and set aside to cool.
5. When cool enough to touch, cut into 1/2 inch thick diagonal slices. Place sliced biscotti on cookie sheet, and bake an additional 5 to 7 minutes on each side, or until toasted and crispy.

CANDIED ALMONDS

Servings: 8 | Prep: 5m | Cooks: 15m | Total: 35m

NUTRITION FACTS

Calories: 304 | Carbohydrates: 32.7g | Fat: 18g | Protein: 7.6g | Cholesterol: 0mg

INGREDIENTS

- 1/2 cup water
- 1 tablespoon ground cinnamon
- 1 cup white sugar
- 2 cups whole almonds

DIRECTIONS

1. Combine the water, sugar, and cinnamon in a saucepan over medium heat; bring to a boil; add the almonds. Cook and stir the mixture until the liquid evaporates and leaves a syrup-like coating on the almonds. Pour the almonds onto a baking sheet lined with waxed paper. Separate almonds using forks. Allow to cool about 15 minutes.

ZESTY PORCUPINE MEATBALLS

Servings: 5 | Prep: 20m | Cooks: 20m | Total: 40m

NUTRITION FACTS

Calories: 408 | Carbohydrates: 32.4g | Fat: 21.6g | Protein: 20.6g | Cholesterol: 105mg

INGREDIENTS

- 1 egg
- 1 teaspoon onion salt
- 2 (10.75 ounce) cans condensed tomato soup
- 1/4 teaspoon ground black pepper
- 1/4 cup instant rice
- 1 pound lean ground beef
- 1/4 cup chopped onion
- 1/4 cup Worcestershire sauce
- 1 tablespoon chopped fresh parsley

DIRECTIONS

1. Lightly beat egg with a fork, then add a heaping tablespoon of the soup and mix lightly. Mix in rice, onion, parsley, onion salt and pepper. Stir in the ground beef and mix well with hands. From mixture into 1 1/2 inch round meatballs.
2. Coat a large skillet over medium heat with cooking spray. Cook meatballs and brown on all sides.
3. Combine remaining soup with Worcestershire (you can increase or decrease Worcestershire to your liking), stir until smooth, then spoon over meatballs. Cover with lid and simmer for 20 to 30 minutes, stirring every few minutes.

ISLAND KIELBASA IN A SLOW COOKER

Servings: 6 | Prep: 10m | Cooks: 5h | Total: 5h10m

NUTRITION FACTS

Calories: 866 | Carbohydrates: 107.5g | Fat: 41.6g | Protein: 20.3g | Cholesterol: 100mg

INGREDIENTS

- 2 pounds kielbasa sausage, sliced into 1/2 inch pieces
- 2 cups brown sugar
- 2 cups ketchup
- 1 (15 ounce) can pineapple chunks, undrained

DIRECTIONS

1. Place the sausage, ketchup, sugar and pineapple in the slow cooker and mix together.
2. Cook on low setting for 5 to 6 hours, until sausage is cooked through.

SPICED SLOW COOKER APPLESAUCE

Servings: 8 | Prep: 10m | Cooks: 6h30m | Total: 6h40m

NUTRITION FACTS

Calories: 150 | Carbohydrates: 39.4g | Fat: 0.2g | Protein: 0.4g | Cholesterol: 0mg

INGREDIENTS

- 8 apples - peeled, cored, and thinly sliced
- 3/4 cup packed brown sugar
- 1/2 cup water
- 1/2 teaspoon pumpkin pie spice

DIRECTIONS

1. Combine the apples and water in a slow cooker; cook on Low for 6 to 8 hours. Stir in the brown sugar and pumpkin pie spice; continue cooking another 30 minutes.

BRAZILIAN WHITE RICE

Servings: 8 | Prep: 15m | Cooks: 30m | Total: 45m

NUTRITION FACTS

Calories: 201 | Carbohydrates: 37.5g | Fat: 3.7g | Protein: 3.4g | Cholesterol: 0mg

INGREDIENTS

- 2 cups long-grain white rice
- 2 tablespoons vegetable oil
- 2 tablespoons minced onion
- 1 teaspoon salt
- 2 cloves garlic, minced
- 4 cups hot water

DIRECTIONS

1. Place the rice in a colander and rinse thoroughly with cold water; set aside.
2. Heat the oil in a saucepan over medium heat. Cook the onion in the oil for one minute. Stir in the garlic and cook until the garlic is golden brown. Add the rice and salt and cook and stir until the rice begins to brown. Pour hot water over rice mixture and stir. Reduce heat to low, cover the saucepan, and allow to simmer until the water has been absorbed, 20 to 25 minutes.

TOFU AND VEGGIES IN PEANUT SAUCE

Servings: 4 | Prep: 10m | Cooks: 10m | Total: 20m

NUTRITION FACTS

Calories: 443 | Carbohydrates: 24g | Fat: 29.9g | Protein: 29g | Cholesterol: 0mg

INGREDIENTS

- 1 tablespoon peanut oil
- 1/2 cup hot water
- 1 small head broccoli, chopped
- 2 tablespoons vinegar
- 1 small red bell pepper, chopped
- 2 tablespoons soy sauce
- 5 fresh mushrooms, sliced
- 1 1/2 tablespoons molasses
- 1 pound firm tofu, cubed
- ground cayenne pepper to taste
- 1/2 cup peanut butter

DIRECTIONS

1. Heat oil in a large skillet or wok over medium-high heat. Saute broccoli, red bell pepper, mushrooms and tofu for 5 minutes.
2. In a small bowl combine peanut butter, hot water, vinegar, soy sauce, molasses and cayenne pepper. Pour over vegetables and tofu. Simmer for 3 to 5 minutes, or until vegetables are tender crisp.

APPLE BUNDT CAKE

Servings: 12 | Prep: 30m | Cooks: 1h | Total: 2h | Additional: 30m

Calories: 523 | Carbohydrates: 66.3g | Fat: 26.7g | Protein: 6.9g | Cholesterol: 62mg

INGREDIENTS

- 2 cups apples - peeled, cored and diced
- 1 cup vegetable oil
- 1 tablespoon white sugar
- 1/4 cup orange juice
- 1 teaspoon ground cinnamon
- 2 1/2 teaspoons vanilla extract
- 3 cups all-purpose flour
- 4 eggs
- 3 teaspoons baking powder
- 1 cup chopped walnuts
- 1/2 teaspoon salt
- 1/4 cup confectioners' sugar for dusting
- 2 cups white sugar

DIRECTIONS

1. Preheat oven to 350 degrees F (175 degrees C). Grease and flour a 10 inch Bundt or tube pan. In a medium bowl, combine the diced apples, 1 tablespoon white sugar and 1 teaspoon cinnamon; set aside. Sift together the flour, baking powder and salt; set aside.
2. In a large bowl, combine 2 cups white sugar, oil, orange juice, vanilla and eggs. Beat at high speed until smooth. Stir in flour mixture. Fold in chopped walnuts.
3. Pour 1/3 of the batter into prepared pan. Sprinkle with 1/2 of the apple mixture. Alternate layers of batter and filling, ending with batter.
4. Bake in preheated oven for 55 to 60 minutes, or until the top springs back when lightly touched. Let cool in pan for 10 minutes, then turn out onto a wire rack and cool completely. Sprinkle with confectioners' sugar.

SLOW COOKER GREEN BEANS, HAM AND POTATOES

Servings: 10 | Prep: 30m | Cooks: 4h | Total: 4h30m

NUTRITION FACTS

Calories: 200 | Carbohydrates: 20.6g | Fat: 9g | Protein: 10.2g | Cholesterol: 29mg

INGREDIENTS

- 2 pounds fresh green beans, rinsed and trimmed
- 1 teaspoon onion powder
- 1 large onion, chopped
- 1 teaspoon seasoning salt
- 3 ham hocks
- 1 tablespoon chicken bouillon granules
- 1 1/2 pounds new potatoes, quartered
- ground black pepper to taste
- 1 teaspoon garlic powder

DIRECTIONS

1. Halve beans if they are large, place in a slow cooker with water to barely cover, and add onion and ham hocks. Cover, and cook on High until simmering. Reduce heat to Low, and cook for 2 to 3 hours, or until beans are crisp but not done.
2. Add potatoes, and cook for another 45 minutes. While potatoes are cooking, remove ham hocks from slow cooker, and remove meat from bones. Chop or shred meat, and return to slow cooker. Season with garlic powder, onion powder, seasoning salt, bouillon, and pepper. Cook until potatoes are done, then adjust seasoning to taste
3. To serve, use a slotted spoon to put beans, potatoes, and ham into a serving dish with a little broth.

GRILLED SALMON

Servings: 6 | Prep: 10m | Cooks: 20m | Total: 6h30m

NUTRITION FACTS

Calories: 233 | Carbohydrates: 2.9g | Fat: 17.6g | Protein: 15.3g | Cholesterol: 44mg

INGREDIENTS

- 4 (4 ounce) fillets salmon
- 1 clove garlic, minced
- 1/4 cup peanut oil
- 3/4 teaspoon ground ginger
- 2 tablespoons soy sauce
- 1/2 teaspoon crushed red pepper flakes
- 2 tablespoons balsamic vinegar
- 1/2 teaspoon sesame oil
- 2 tablespoons thinly sliced green onion
- 1/8 teaspoon salt
- 1 1/2 teaspoons brown sugar

DIRECTIONS

1. Whisk together peanut oil, soy sauce, balsamic vinegar, green onions, garlic, brown sugar, ginger, red chile flakes, sesame oil, and salt. Place fish in a glass dish, and pour marinade over all. Cover with plastic wrap, and refrigerate for 4 to 6 hours.
2. Preheat barbecue or gas grill.
3. Oil the grill rack, and adjust height to 5 inches from coals. Remove salmon from marinade, and place on grill. Grill for 10 minutes per inch of thickness, measured at thickest part, or until fish just flakes when tested with a fork. Turn halfway through cooking.

BOW TIE PASTA WITH SAUSAGE AND SWEET PEPPERS

Servings: 4 | Prep: 10m | Cooks: 25m | Total: 35m

NUTRITION FACTS

Calories: 489 | Carbohydrates: 48g | Fat: 22.9g | Protein: 23.3g | Cholesterol: 45mg

INGREDIENTS

- 1 pound Italian sausage, cut into 1/2 inch pieces
- 1/2 cup beef broth
- 2 green bell peppers, chopped
- 1/4 teaspoon ground black pepper

- 8 ounces farfalle pasta

DIRECTIONS

1. Bring a large pot of lightly salted water to a boil. Add pasta and cook for 8 to 10 minutes or until al dente; drain.
2. While pasta is cooking, cook sausage and peppers in large skillet over medium heat until sausage is brown and juices run clear. Drain sausage mixture and return it to the pan. Pour in the broth, season with black pepper and bring to a boil.
3. Toss pasta with sausage sauce and serve.

AMERICAN CHOP SUEY

Servings: 5 | Prep: 5m | Cooks: 25m | Total: 30m

NUTRITION FACTS

Calories: 664 | Carbohydrates: 85.1g | Fat: 22g | Protein: 30g | Cholesterol: 68mg

INGREDIENTS

- 1 (16 ounce) package uncooked elbow macaroni
- 2 (10.75 ounce) cans condensed tomato soup
- 1 pound lean ground beef
- salt and pepper to taste
- 1 onion, chopped

DIRECTIONS

1. Cook macaroni according to package directions.
2. Meanwhile, in a separate large skillet over medium high heat, saute the ground beef and the onion for 5 to 10 minutes, or until meat is browned and crumbly. Drain thoroughly and leave the meat and onion in the skillet. Pour the two cans of tomato soup into the skillet and stir well to combine.
3. When noodles are done, drain thoroughly and return noodles to the pot. Add the hamburger mixture from the skillet to the pot. Mix well and season with salt and pepper to taste.

FRIED OKRA

Servings: 4 | Prep: 15m | Cooks: 15m | Total: 30m

NUTRITION FACTS

Calories: 394 | Carbohydrates: 29g | Fat: 29.2g | Protein: 4.7g | Cholesterol: 46mg

INGREDIENTS

- 10 pods okra, sliced in 1/4 inch pieces
- 1/4 teaspoon salt
- 1 egg, beaten
- 1/4 teaspoon ground black pepper
- 1 cup cornmeal
- 1/2 cup vegetable oil

DIRECTIONS

1. In a small bowl, soak okra in egg for 5 to 10 minutes. In a medium bowl, combine cornmeal, salt, and pepper.
2. Heat oil in a large skillet over medium-high heat. Dredge okra in the cornmeal mixture, coating evenly. Carefully place okra in hot oil; stir continuously. Reduce heat to medium when okra first starts to brown, and cook until golden. Drain on paper towels.

RAMJAM CHICKEN

Servings: 8 | Prep: 20m | Cooks: 15m | Total: 3h55m | Additional: 3h

NUTRITION FACTS

Calories: 303 | Carbohydrates: 1.5g | Fat: 9.1g | Protein: 49.6g | Cholesterol: 134mg

INGREDIENTS

- 1/4 cup soy sauce
- 1 teaspoon grated fresh ginger root
- 3 tablespoons dry white wine
- 1 clove garlic, crushed
- 2 tablespoons lemon juice
- 1/4 teaspoon onion powder
- 2 tablespoons vegetable oil
- 1 pinch ground black pepper
- 3/4 teaspoon dried Italian-style seasoning
- 8 skinless, boneless chicken breast halves - cut into strips

DIRECTIONS

1. In a large, resealable plastic bag, combine the soy sauce, wine, lemon juice, oil, Italian-style seasoning, ginger, garlic, onion powder, and ground black pepper. Place chicken in the bag. Seal, and let marinate in the refrigerator for at least 3 hours, or overnight.
2. Preheat an outdoor grill for medium-high heat.
3. Thread the chicken onto skewers, and set aside. Pour marinade into a small saucepan, and bring to a boil over high heat.
4. Lightly oil the grill grate. Cook chicken on the prepared grill for approximately 8 minutes per side, basting with the sauce several times. Chicken is done when juices run clear.